Parent Hacks

134 Genius Shortcuts for Life with Kids

By Asha Dornfest

Workman Publishing | New York

To Caron Arnold, Sara Carlstead Brumfield, Kara Hagen, Tracy Hengst, Adrienne Jones, Jim Jones, Elana Kehoe, Stu Mark, Rob Monroe, Duane Morin, Heather Petit, Jill Pohl, Kendra Riemermann, Marjorie Wheeler, Homa Woodrum, and the readers of ParentHacks.com. This book and my gratitude are yours. *We made this together.*

In addition to the Parent Hacks community, I'd like to thank the following people for letting me include their hacks: Amy Storch, writing for AlphaMom.com (hack #2, page 10); Sarah Powers, writing for TheHappiestHome.com (hack #56, page 128); and Kate Canterbury, writing for TheGuavaliciousLife.com (hack #65, page 143).

Copyright © 2016 by Asha Dornfest

Library of Congress Cataloging-in-Publication Data is available.
ISBN 978-0-7611-8431-7

Design by Jean-Marc Troadec
Author photo by Karen Walrond

Workman books are available at special discounts when purchased in bulk for premiums and sales promotions as well as for fund-raising or educational use. Special editions or book excerpts also can be created to specification. For details, contact the Special Sales Director at the address below, or send an email to specialmarkets@workman.com.

Workman Publishing Company, Inc.
225 Varick Street
New York, NY 10014-4381
workman.com

WORKMAN is a registered trademark of Workman Publishing Co., Inc.
PARENT HACKS is a registered trademark of Asha Dornfest.

Printed in China
First printing March 2016

10 9 8 7 6 5 4 3

Contents

Introduction

What comes to mind when you think about hackers? Malevolent creators of computer viruses? Bored coders wreaking havoc on the Internet? These people exist. But there's a larger, more influential group of hackers who use their cleverness and ingenuity for good. You know them. *You're one of them.*

Parents are the smartest, most prolific hackers around. Think about it: When was the last time your day went as expected? Raising kids, particularly in the beginning, is the most seat-of-the-pants job there is. You make it up as you go along, and every now and again, you stumble upon a brilliant solution or shortcut that makes your life easier.

Parent Hacks celebrates those flashes of problem-solving genius.

What's a parent hack? You delight in your kid. Of course you do. But, along with the joy, let's acknowledge that parenting comes with its share of annoyances, dilemmas, and full-on crises, many of which require fast thinking under less-than-ideal circumstances. The diaper explodes when you're miles from a bathroom, and you've forgotten to restock the diaper bag. The kid's fast asleep until the pacifier falls out of his mouth and he wakes up screaming. I'm sure you can come up with a few disaster scenarios of your own. One of them probably occurred earlier today.

A *parent hack* is a creative, unexpected solution to a kid-related problem. It's a clever work-around, an inspired shortcut, a duct-tape-and-chewing-gum-type move that changes the game.

Since 2005, I've made it my job to collect and share parent hacks. In fact, the idea for ParentHacks.com grew out of a single question I desperately needed answered when I was a new parent: *Does someone else know what they're doing?*

"This isn't what I expected." Early parenthood didn't exactly line up with my expectations. I'd assumed raising kids would bear some resemblance to the extensive babysitting I'd done as a teenager. Obviously parenthood was larger in scope and longer in duration (and unpaid), but I was confident my husband, Rael, and I could keep level heads while caring for our children and managing our home.

Instead, the kids were crying, the house was a mess, and I felt like I was drowning. Rael did all he could to help, but I had no idea how to help myself. I loved my family and appreciated our life together, which made my struggle as a new parent all the more fraught.

So I did what had always worked for me in the past: I consulted the experts.

I read every parenting and productivity book I could get my hands on with the assumption (or fervent hope) that other people—more *qualified* people—would have the answer. I adopted time-management systems. I called the pediatrician. I adjusted my communication style. I called my mother. I dropped a few hundred dollars on home-organizing supplies. I called my therapist.

But expert advice didn't fix my new life. If anything, it undermined what little confidence I had. I felt *more* overwhelmed (so much information!) and *less* equipped to handle it. (I must be doing this wrong!) Social media wasn't yet a thing, so with no easy way to compare notes beyond my immediate circle, I was plagued by self-doubt. My unflappable optimism . . . flapped.

I found my tribe online. I discovered blogs. At the time, blogs were new enough that finding them felt like stumbling into a secret world. Parents were taking to the Internet, writing their own stories in real time, unvarnished. I was dazzled. This was *nothing* like the stuff I'd read in parenting books and magazines. And by nature of the format, there was an important extra no book or magazine could offer: *an invitation to respond.*

I immediately jumped in and started blogging. The comment section on my posts (and on other blogs) became my sounding board and my release valve, and readers and blog authors from around the country became my friends. We swapped ideas across time zones, laughed at one another's parenting foibles, and revealed struggles we'd been afraid to admit, sometimes even to ourselves. Local friends thought it was weird that I was talking to people on the Internet, but it felt completely natural to me. I'd found my tribe.

In 2005, I launched Parent Hacks with the idea that a blog could be useful for more than storytelling; it could be a platform for exchanging ideas and tips with other parents. My hope was that if enough of us tossed our "worked for me" discoveries into the pot, we'd be able to learn from one another. One parent's moment of genius could help another parent in a moment of crisis.

I shared what practical advice I had about baby gear, household shortcuts, productivity, and helpful shifts in perspective, and I invited other parents to do the same. Most of my kid-wrangling tips didn't resemble the sweet, soft-focus suggestions I'd read in the magazines. It was more like MacGyver meets *What to Expect When You're Expecting.*

Within months, parents from all over the world were emailing me their tips and discoveries. My in-box was flooded with smart ways to deal with diaper blowouts, leaky sippy cups, picky toddlers, and cluttered homes. A blog post would inspire discussion in the comments, which would lead to new posts and even more interesting conversation.

An intelligent, generous community grew around my blog, and I found myself surrounded by parents who were inventive, kind, and unafraid to admit that, yeah, life with kids is complicated. I still had more questions than answers, and I still felt overwhelmed at times, but I also felt more confident that I'd figure it out as I went along. We all would, together.

You're the expert, even when it doesn't feel like it. My readers taught me something I wish I had known from the start: **Parenting is a series of best guesses.** We rarely feel sure of ourselves. How can we when we're making case-by-case decisions based on spotty data and shifting variables, on too little sleep?

Parent Hacks also proved to me that, without a doubt, we *all* have moments of brilliance. Raising kids reveals our hidden problem-solving ninja. Not every day, not always when we need it, but surely and eventually, we all shine.

The thing is, our flashes of genius are too easily forgotten in the stumble toward bedtime. That's why I started a blog and now have pulled together this book: to save and pass along these gems. This book is crammed with 134 illustrated tips that will make you smack your forehead and wonder, why didn't I think of that?

You'll find tips on a range of topics from late pregnancy to birth and early parenthood, from organizing your home to feeding and clothing your kids and keeping them (relatively) clean and healthy. You'll get ideas for simplifying outings and travel, suggestions for playtime and learning, and tips for managing holidays and special occasions.

You'll also find new and creative uses for items you probably already have in your home.

You deserve a high five. The Parent Hacks community provides something more subtle—but more important—than tips. I call it *microrecognition:* a high five for discovering a solution others have overlooked. A well-deserved pat on the back for the scrappy problem-solving you do every day.

The best thing about parent hacks is that, by definition, there's more than one "right" way to solve a problem. Every family is unique, so just because a parent hack worked for one person that doesn't mean it has to (or should) work for you.

Join the conversation with #parenthacks. The conversation continues and I want you—yes, you—to be a part of it. The next time you hit on a clever solution to a kid-related problem, post a picture on your favorite social platform with #parenthacks. The more we swap our parent hacks, the smarter and more confident we all become.

Even if you think "it's too obvious" or "people will think

this is dumb," share your parent hacks. You never know . . . the simplest ideas are sometimes the ones that change people's lives.

Visit me. ParentHacks.com contains hundreds of hacks that don't appear in the book, plus the latest from me. You can also find me on Facebook, Twitter, and Instagram (@ashadornfest). I'd love to hear from you.

Parenting is the wildest ride we'll ever take. Isn't it good to know we're in this boat—and paddling—together?

Let's get hacking.

WHAT'S YOUR PARENT HACK?
#PARENTHACKS

Chapter 1
Pregnancy & Postpartum

When a new baby arrives, the universe inexplicably shifts in a way that's impossible to understand before you're actually there. How do you anticipate the needs of a small person you've never met?

Despite what you've heard, there's not much you *must* do before your baby arrives. Set up the baby-care basics, write a few thank-you notes, stock the freezer with some simple meals (better yet, let someone else stock it), then enjoy the remainder of your child-free life.

#1

Expand the waistband of your prepregnancy jeans with a ponytail holder.

Skip the maternity waistband extenders—a ponytail holder does the job just as well. Thread a small elastic band through the buttonhole of your pants and then back through itself, creating a slipknot loop. Then stretch it over the button closure.

If the zipper won't stay up, thread a second band through the hole in the zipper pull and loop it over the button.

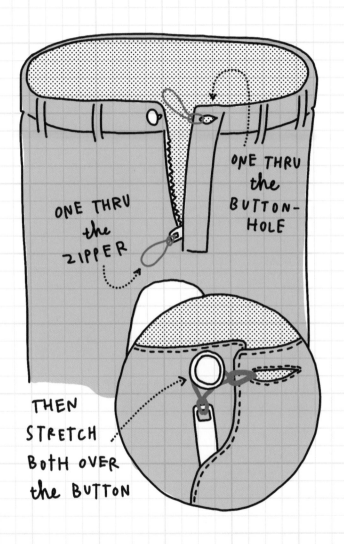

ONE THRU the ZIPPER

ONE THRU the BUTTON-HOLE

THEN STRETCH BOTH OVER the BUTTON

#2

Wear a men's undershirt to add belly coverage to your tops.

Near the end of my pregnancy, I was constantly tugging my maternity T-shirts down in a futile attempt to keep the underside of my belly covered.

The fix: a package of men's tank undershirts. They're cut longer than women's tanks and can be a helpful base layer, providing coverage without feeling bulky or fussy.

UNDERSHIRTS are STRETCHY!

UNDERSHIRTS are LONG!

(and UNDERSHIRTS are CHEAP!)

#3

If your bra no longer fits, wear a bikini top.

Keeping up with the epic body changes of pregnancy can get expensive. Take bras: Your breasts change size and shape more than once during pregnancy and postpartum. Bra extenders work for a while (buy them at a maternity store), but are sometimes outgrown. Sports bras are more forgiving, but are difficult to get on and off.

For some, a string-tie bikini top provides all the necessary coverage, support, and comfort during one or more of these stages.

WEAR a
BIKINI TOP
INSTEAD
of a BRA
for
BEACH VIBES

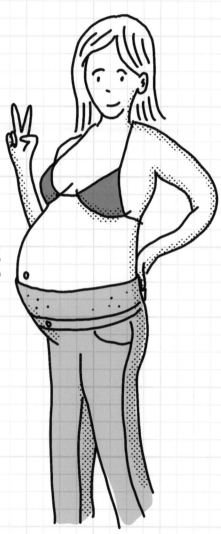

#4

Take pictures of gifts with their givers as a thank-you note reminder.

Parenting truth: Your organizational skills are most needed at the very moment when your brain has the lowest capacity for them.

To keep track of gifts and their givers: Write the giver's name in big letters on the back of the card or packing slip. Then place it next to the opened gift and snap a picture.

If you're doing this at the baby shower, have a friend snap a picture of you, the gift giver, and the opened gift. The photos serve as a digital inventory as well as a lovely memento of the occasion.

SNAP a PIC for a VISUAL REMINDER

* INSTAGRAM OPTIONAL

10 baby gear items you don't need
(with smarter alternatives)

When people ask if you're "ready for the baby," they usually mean, "Do you have all the stuff?" People assume that babies require a mountain of specialized gear, but in the beginning, all you need are a few basic care and clothing items, a sturdy car seat and stroller frame, a carrier, a breast pump and/or bottles, and a safe, comfortable place for your baby to sleep. As your baby gets older, you'll naturally become more adept at figuring out what you need, what to buy, and what to borrow. In the meantime, here are 10 common registry items that you can do without.

1 **Diaper pail.** You'll dispose of many, *many* dirty diapers in the first few years. Do you need a specialized receptacle? No. If you're using a cloth diaper service, they'll provide a pail. If not, a lined garbage can (preferably with a foot pedal) will do fine. With disposables, get rid of them as you go. Flush what solids you can, seal the diaper in a used plastic bag, and toss it in your outside garbage.

2 Changing table.

Place a changing pad on top of a dresser, or spread a waterproof mat on the bed, clothes dryer, or floor. Or choose furniture you can repurpose, such as a rolling kitchen cart (with locking wheels) or a small computer desk.

3 Wipe warmer.

Just no.

4 Fancy crib bedding.

All you need for your baby's crib is a fitted sheet and a waterproof mattress protector. That said, if you're excited about decorating the crib, don't let practicality get in the way of a lovely experience.

5 Special laundry detergent.

Any mild, fragrance-free detergent will do the job.

6 Baby toiletries.

Mild soap, shampoo, and moisturizer work for everyone in the family.

7 Diaper stacker.

Keep a small basket of diapers near the changing area and hang the diaper stacker that came with the crib bedding set in the closet to hold sheets, blankets, or stuffed animals.

8 Baby bathtub.

Bathe your baby in the sink. As your baby gets bigger and can sit up, she can graduate to a plastic laundry basket in the regular bathtub.

9 Nursing clothing.

After a few weeks of breast-feeding, *everything* is nursing clothing. Stretchy knit tops and button-front cardigans are especially forgiving.

10 Nursing cover-ups.

Within a relatively short time, you'll figure out how to discreetly nurse your baby. Till then, if you're feeling exposed, toss a light receiving blanket over your shoulder (or knot two corners together and drape it around your neck).

#5

Sleep more comfortably with a **DIY pregnancy pillow.**

Can't sleep with what feels like a bowling ball attached to your abdomen? Hugging a body pillow while lying on your side helps. Before you invest in a special pregnancy support pillow ($$$), why not make your own?

Stuff two soft standard-size bed pillows into a single king-size pillow sham. Rearrange the pillows inside so that you (and your belly) feel comfortable while lying on your side.

KING-SIZE
SHAM

2 STANDARD-
SIZE PILLOWS

#6

Carry an adult diaper in case your water breaks before labor.

"Your water breaking" sounds far more dramatic than it actually is. There's no pain, but, should it happen, you've got an awkward mess on your hands (actually, your legs).

No big deal. Tuck an adult diaper into your bag (if you're really worried, wear it instead of regular underwear). You probably won't need it, but if you do, you'll be glad you thought ahead.

How to use up the rest of the adult diapers in the package? They'll come in handy during postpartum recovery (see page 23).

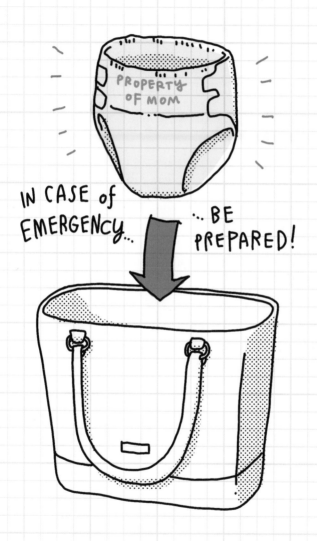

IN CASE of EMERGENCY...

...BE PREPARED!

PROPERTY OF MOM

9 nonessential items you'll be glad you packed in your hospital bag

There's not much you need that the hospital won't provide or someone can't fetch for you. Even so, consider packing some familiar comforts that aren't strictly necessary. When you're stuck in the hospital in the midst of hormonal bliss/chaos, having a few luxuries goes a long way.

1 A light, inexpensive bathrobe. It will feel like heaven after hours in a hospital gown. It may get messed up (one word: FLUIDS), but your comfort is worth it.

2 Ponytail holders or a headband. If you have long hair, you'll want to keep it out of your face. Or this might be the moment for that short haircut you've been thinking about.

3 Cozy footwear you don't mind throwing away. Fuzzy socks and comfy slippers are warm hugs for your feet.

4 Favorite toiletries and cosmetics. This is less about vanity and more about physical and psychological comfort. The smell of your favorite conditioner may add a whiff of normalcy to the postpartum whirlwind.

5 Dry shampoo. You may have to wait a day or two till you can take a shower. Dry shampoo does a remarkable job of refreshing your hair and scalp.

6 A towel. Hospital towels are notoriously thin and scratchy. Once you're able to shower, you'll want a soft, full-size towel. Bring one you won't mind leaving behind.

7 Nursing pillow. It takes a while to get the hang of breast-feeding. You can prop yourself (and your baby) up with a hospital pillow, but you'll probably prefer the comfort and shape of a nursing pillow.

8 An adult diaper. As if childbirth weren't dramatic enough, you also get to experience postpartum flow that rivals the heaviest, longest period you've ever had. Oh, joy. Many moms who've gone before you swear that an adult diaper is the best tool during this . . . period.

9 Stretch pants and a roomy top for going home. Anything stretchy, washable, and comfortable will do.

Cabbage leaf compresses help relieve swollen breasts and feet.

When nursing, it takes time for milk production to regulate, and for some, engorgement (painfully full breasts) complicates the early weeks. An age-old remedy is in the produce section: cabbage leaves.

To make a compress, remove a few leaves from a cabbage. Crush the veins with a rolling pin and then drape the leaves over your breasts for 20 to 30 minutes, or until they wilt. Repeat three to four times each day until swelling subsides (a day or two).

PEEL OFF *the* CABBAGE LEAF

ROLL OUT *the* LEAF

APPLY & RELAX

Freeze a sanitary pad to help heal after childbirth.

After a vaginal childbirth, the delicate tissues down there need time to heal. For a cool compress that stays put, dampen (don't soak) a sanitary pad and freeze it.

Wear a maternity jacket over the front carrier.

The easiest way to transport and/or calm a newborn is to "wear" him in a carrier. In chilly weather, keep warm by zipping your maternity jacket around you both.

ZIP
&
SNUGGLE

#10

Use **toothpaste** to mark the spot for picture frame nail holes.

Here's a trick for quickly and accurately hanging art in the baby's nursery (or any room, really!). Dab a spot of toothpaste on the serrated hanger on the back of the frame, then press the picture to the wall. You'll leave a little spot of white paste showing you where to place the nail.

If the frame uses hanging wire, hold the wire taut and place the toothpaste at the center point, hold the picture up to the wall, and gently press.

1. APPLY a DAB of TOOTHPASTE to the BACK...

2. PLACE the FRAME on the WALL...

3. PUT YOUR ANCHOR in at the RIGHT SPOT the FIRST TIME!

FOR MORE THAN JUST DIRTY BOTTOMS,
BABY WIPES
are the PERFECT ANSWER to SO MUCH of EVERYDAY LIFE'S GRIT and GRIME.

REMOVE TEMPORARY TATTOOS

REMOVE DEODORANT STAINS

WIPE DOWN STICKY RESTAURANT TABLES

PET PAW CLEANER

HOUSEPLANT CLEANER

DASHBOARD CLEANER

DAMP SWIFFER INSERT

FACE WIPE & MAKEUP REMOVER

CLEAN CAR SEATS

REMOVE CRAYON on a WALL

5 alternatives to a traditional baby book

Despite our best intentions to jot down all those milestones and firsts, baby arrives, life happens, and it all goes south.

Don't let baby-book guilt stop you from making a record. It will be treasured, no matter what. Here are a few tips for taking notes as life flies by. Use them to fill a baby book later on, or replace the book altogether.

1 A calendar. Keep a datebook by the changing table and jot a few notes and observations into it every day.

2 Index cards. Keep a box of index cards nearby. Whenever you feel inspired, write a sentence or two on a card and date it.

3 A notebook. Keep a small journal with you for quick notes. Later you can tape drawings and pictures into the notebook, too.

4 A box. Throw notes, pictures, and keepsakes into a box. Date everything.

5 Your phone. The pictures, videos, and notes on your phone will be automatically dated, and you can download and print (or post) the highlights later on. (Be sure to back up your data.)

Chapter 2
Organizing Time & Space

Your baby is no longer an amorphous belly lump. He's now a breathing, eating, pooping (and hopefully sleeping) human being who's taken over your home and your heart.

For such small people, children have an impact on every room in the house. This calls for some serious organization and time management. As it happens, you now have less time to think about how to use your time, and less mental real estate to devote to your actual real estate.

The goal isn't domestic perfection and robotlike efficiency—it's a comfortable refuge and time to enjoy it.

Sort your to-do list by the time it takes to complete each job.

A written to-do list is the best way to give your beleaguered memory a break.

Give each to-do list item a time-based label ("5 minutes," "15 minutes," or whatever intervals work for you). Electronic to-do apps let you categorize tasks, but if you prefer a paper to-do list, just pencil a time label next to each task.

When you find yourself with a snatch of time, scan your list quickly to see which tasks you can reasonably complete.

Organize electronics charger cables with toilet paper tubes.

Parenthood has probably added to your already overflowing collection of cords. Instead of throwing them into a drawer, coil each cable and stuff it into a labeled cardboard toilet paper tube.

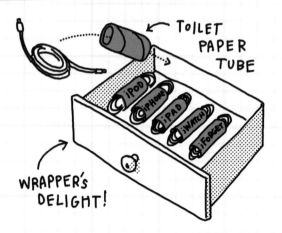

TOILET PAPER TUBE

WRAPPER'S DELIGHT!

Turn a bookshelf into a hanging wardrobe.

Short on closet space? Turn an adjustable bookshelf into a hanging wardrobe: Remove a shelf and fit a spring-loaded tension rod inside.

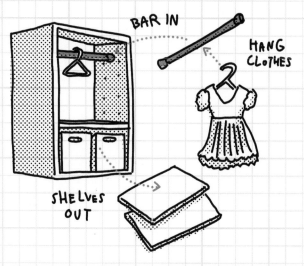

BAR IN

HANG CLOTHES

SHELVES OUT

19 cleaning & organizing projects that take 10 minutes or less

Swaths of uninterrupted time are a thing of the past. One of the best skills you can develop as a new parent is the ability to knock off short tasks and to break larger tasks into 10-minute chunks. That way, you can chip away at those nagging chores even when you're not sure about how much free time you have left. Set a timer or see what you can get done while the microwave reheats your lunch—you'll be amazed by what you can accomplish. A few suggestions to get you started:

1 **Open** the mail, write the due dates on bills, place them in a file folder, and recycle the envelopes.

2 **Gather** the old newspapers, magazines, and flyers around your house and recycle them.

3 **Sort** and refold all the clothes in just one of your dresser drawers.

4 **Wipe** or brush the crumbs and other debris out of the kitchen cutlery drawer.

5 **Empty** all the wastebaskets in the house.

6 **Sweep** and tidy the entryway (you'll feel better about the whole house).

7 **Wipe down** the bathroom sink, counter, and toilet.

8 **Open** your file drawer, remove a single file, organize the contents, shred any outdated materials, then put back the rest.

9 **Recycle** the mismatched and throwaway plastic containers taking up space in your kitchen cabinets.

10 **Straighten up** a single bookshelf.

11 **Clear off** or neaten the coffee table.

12 **Tidy** the trunk and interior of your car and wipe down the dashboard.

13 **Edit** and organize photos (printed or digital) for 10 minutes.

14 **Sort** your email in-box.

15 **Dampen** a paper towel and wipe the inside of the microwave.

16 **Organize** the cabinet under your bathroom or kitchen sink.

17 **Clear out** the diaper bag or backpack.

18 **Make** the bed. (Bonus: You can even treat yourself to a fresh set of sheets!)

19 **Clean out** and wipe down your refrigerator crisper drawers.

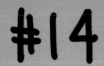

#14

Batch-sign and -address birthday cards in advance.

My mom and aunt have the amazing ability to mail birthday cards to everyone in the family on time. Alas, that skill skipped a generation, and I've spent years feeling bad about belated birthday greetings. This system puts an end to birthday card guilt.

Buy birthday cards four or five at a time. When you have some downtime, write the cards out to their intended recipients. Sign, seal, address, and stamp the cards, then file them in a place you'll remember.

Next, set an alert to remind you to mail the card three to four days before the recipient's birthday.

① BUY in BULK

② WRITE in BULK

③ NEVER FORGET

SEND DAD'S CARD
OK

THE SMALL, CLEAR, GRIDDED POCKETS in a

HANGING SHOE ORGANIZER

are GREAT for COLLECTING SMALL ITEMS. JUST KEEP the LOWER POCKETS OUT of REACH of KIDS (or FILLED with KID-SAFE STUFF).

SINGLE-SERVE SNACK PACKS

HAIR ACCESSORIES

SEASONAL GEAR

GIFT WRAP STUFF

ELECTRONIC GADGETS & CHARGERS

CARD GAMES

LAUNDRY SUPPLIES

SMALL TOY COLLECTIONS

HOME REPAIR

SOCKS & TIGHTS

KITCHEN GADGETS

BILLS & MAILING SUPPLIES

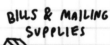

DRESS-UP JEWELRY & ACCESSORIES

BABY-CARE SUPPLIES

WATER BOTTLES

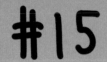

#15

Remove pet fur from furniture with a squeegee and a pair of dishwashing gloves.

Nothing attracts pet fur like the pant knees of a crawling baby or the sticky hands of a toddler. Give your carpet or upholstery a few swipes with a rubber window squeegee. Pet hair will gather into a pile that's easier to pick up or vacuum away.

For those spots the squeegee can't reach, don a pair of dishwashing gloves to rub and gather the rest of the fur.

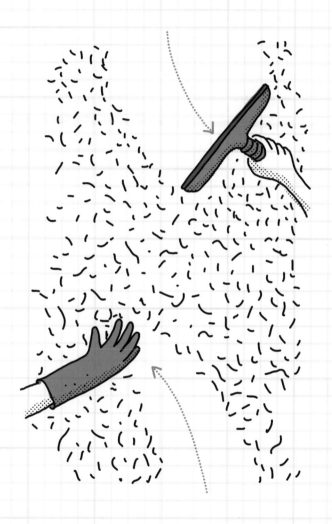

8 answers to the question "How can I help?"

People want to know what they can do to help, but you may be too tired or hormone-addled to come up with an answer.

The next time someone asks, point to this page.

1 Bring a meal. The best meals come in a single pan or pot, are freezable, and make good leftovers. Then again, *any* meal someone else prepares is the best meal, especially if you can eat it one-handed. *Tip:* If friends bring meals in containers that need to be returned, label them (painter's tape and a permanent marker) right away or transfer the meal into your own container so they can take theirs home.

2 Buy groceries. Keep your grocery list posted on a whiteboard in the kitchen or in an electronic version you can share. Ask your friends to text you from the store so you can send them your list, or message them a picture of the whiteboard. And keep in mind: One cannot live on enchiladas alone. Ask your friends to pick up some dried fruit and nuts or washed and cut fresh fruit and vegetables for salads and snacking.

3 **Do dishes.** Awkward as it may seem to ask friends to clean, doing the dishes is something anyone can do, and it's time-limited enough to delegate. Just think how wonderful it will be to walk into a clean kitchen. Remember: Your friends *want to help*.

4 **Do laundry.** The great thing about laundry (in this case) is that there's always some waiting to be done. Friends can throw a load in the washer or dryer, fold dry clothes, or change and wash the towels.

5 **Address and stamp envelopes.** Those baby announcements and thank-you notes aren't going to send themselves. Let your friends pitch in with the stamping, sealing, and/or addressing of envelopes.

6 **Walk the dog.** Or pet the cat. Pets are bound to be confused and possibly agitated by your home's new occupant and rhythms. Let your pet-loving guests offer as much extra attention as they are willing to give.

7 **Take siblings on an outing.** Older brothers and sisters will love special and celebratory treatment that's "just for big kids."

8 **Watch the baby.** Ask for an hour, so you can take a nap. Or 15 minutes, so you can shower. Or five minutes, so you can simply have a moment to yourself.

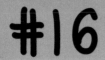
#16

Install a tension rod inside the shower to increase storage and drying space.

If your bathtub ledges are overflowing with toys, shampoo, and soggy washcloths, install a spring-loaded shower curtain rod inside the bath, high enough that it's out of grabbing and head-bumping range. Use it as a drip-dry rack for swimsuits and delicates, and hang lightweight plastic baskets from the rod with shower curtain hooks to hold bath toys.

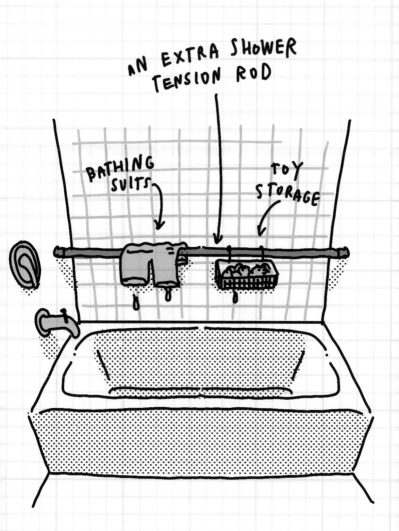

AN EXTRA SHOWER
TENSION ROD

BATHING
SUITS

TOY
STORAGE

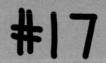
#17

Create a toy library to keep teddies and trucks from taking over your house.

A toy library keeps toys organized, adds variety to playtime, and makes it easier for older kids to clean up after themselves.

Separate toys by category (blocks, cars, dolls, etc.) and designate one bin for each. (Choose clear plastic bins so it's easy to see what's inside.)

When it's time to play, "check out" toys from the library and move them to a small basket in the living room (or wherever playtime is happening). When it's time to play with something new, "check in" the old toy.

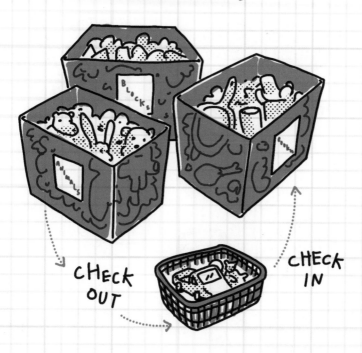

IF MASKING TAPE *and* STICKY NOTES HAD a LOVE CHILD,

PAINTER'S TAPE

WOULD BE IT. IT'S VISIBLE, EASY to TEAR, and STAYS PUT—BUT LEAVES NO RESIDUE BEHIND.

LABEL LEFTOVERS

LABEL CORDS & WIRES

TV

STEREO

LABEL BELONGINGS

SEAL SNACK BAGS

HANG PARTY DECOR

3

ENTERTAIN TODDLERS
on a PLANE
(MORE FUN
THAN YOU
THINK)

MARK the
"HOT ZONE"
AROUND the STOVE
or GRILL

BABYPROOF
a HOTEL ROOM

power outlet

drawers

FIX a RIPPED
DIAPER TAB

INDOOR FLOOR GAMES!

mazes

balance beams

hopscotch

racetrack

beanbag toss

Organize coloring supplies with a dish drainer.

Slide coloring books into the slots of a plastic dish drainer and crayons and markers into the attached cutlery drying cup—they'll be contained, ordered, and easy to transport.

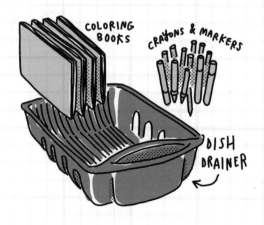

COLORING BOOKS

CRAYONS & MARKERS

DISH DRAINER

Contain books in a shoe box or wall-mounted file holder.

Corral board books in plastic shoe boxes or attach a plastic file holder to the wall to create "pocket" storage for a few books.

the MESS

the SOLUTION

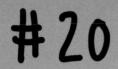

#20

Set a reminder to revisit fun activities you've missed.

There's rarely enough time to do all of the fun things that catch your eye. Instead of fretting about what you're missing, make a note in your calendar to try again another time.

Let's say you come across a new local park: You want to stop and look around, but your kid's pitching a fit. Add an appointment to your calendar for the following week so you'll remember to plan for a visit. If the activity is seasonal (for a specific holiday, say), make a note to look for it next year.

This hack also works for recipes to try and events to attend, with a reminder to purchase supplies or tickets ahead of time.

7 chores your toddler can do right now

That's right, I just used the words "chores" and "toddler" in the same sentence. Toddlers *can* do chores! Not *well,* but that's not the point. Chores are the best way to tap into a toddler's natural excitement about growing up. Giving toddlers real work demonstrates that everyone in the family can pitch in, and that they are capable little humans.

Let your toddler do these jobs:

1 **Wipe down** surfaces with a damp cloth.

2 **Throw** dirty clothes in the hamper.

3 **Put** toys or books away in a basket.

4 **Hang** a jacket or backpack on a low hook.

5 **Stow** all shoes in a basket or bin.

6 **Carry** dirty dishes to the kitchen.

7 **Water** outdoor plants with a small watering can.

Chapter 3
Poop, Pee & Potty

What goes in must come out. And it keeps coming out.

The job of butt-wiper, diaper-wrangler, and potty-cajoler is a long and storied one, and it's all yours. Accept this role and you can (almost) enjoy it—plus you'll be able to entertain friends with poop-related stories for years.

Here are some smart ways to get a better handle on the stuff you'd rather not handle.

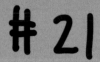

21

Put multiple covers on the changing pad.

Dirty changing pad covers are inevitable. Plan ahead and layer them. When one cover gets dirty, peel it off to reveal a new, clean pad underneath.

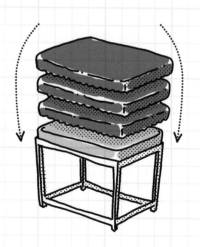

22

Try this trick for tightening too-large disposable diapers.

No one tells you that babies can outgrow one disposable diaper size before fitting into the next. To tighten the waist and close the gap at the legs, angle the tabs down rather than straight across.

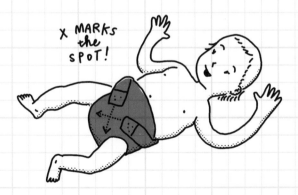

X MARKS the SPOT!

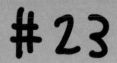

Repair broken diaper tabs with adhesive bandages.

The fasteners on disposable diapers are pretty reliable, but a single malfunction is all it takes to ruin a day. An adhesive bandage is sticky and strong enough for the job, at least until you get home. Another option: painter's tape (see also pages 52–53).

ADHESIVE BANDAGES

PAINTER'S TAPE

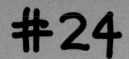

#24

Use a maxi pad as a disposable diaper extender.

There will be long, wet nights when a disposable diaper requires some backup. The fact is, your kid will eventually out-pee a technologically advanced moisture-absorption device.

For those times, call in the big guns: *feminine protection.* An extra-long maxi pad provides the reinforcement a diaper needs to make it through till morning.

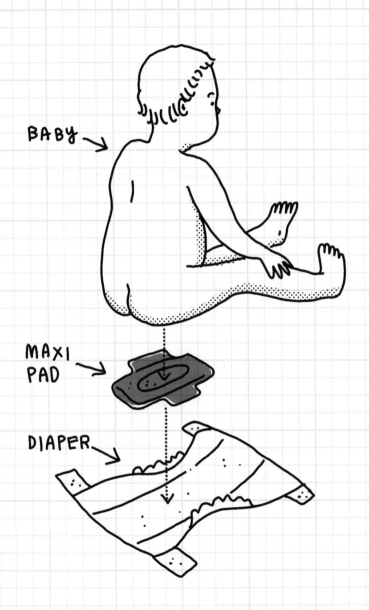

BABY

MAXI
PAD

DIAPER

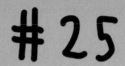

 # 25

After a diaper blowout, take the onesie off top to bottom.

A diaper blowout is a leak so spectacularly messy it requires a head-to-toe cleanup. You may know this already.

If a blowout occurs while your baby is wearing a onesie, stretch open the neckline, peel it down over your baby's shoulders, and then off at the feet—*way* more pleasant for everyone involved.

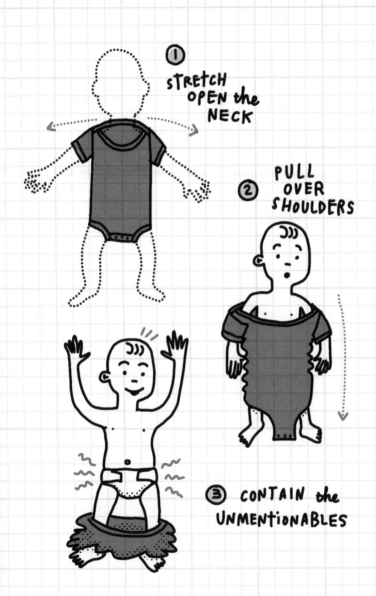

① STRETCH OPEN the NECK

② PULL OVER SHOULDERS

③ CONTAIN the UNMENTIONABLES

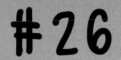
#26

Use a lint roller to remove debris from the bottom of the diaper bag.

For the next couple of years, you'll live out of your diaper bag. What starts as a neatly organized tote inevitably morphs into a catch-all for crumbly snacks, forgotten bottles, dirty clothes, and random toys.

Between washings, swipe the inside of the bag with a lint roller to catch crumbs, fluff, and other flotsam.

KEEP
on
ROLLING

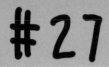
Reuse a peri bottle as a diaper sprayer.

Rather than install a toilet sprayer, use a postpartum peri bottle (or any plastic squeeze bottle) to spray excess poop out of cloth diapers.

PERI BOTTLE

BLASTING POOP!

Snap onesie flaps over the shoulder during potty visits.

If your potty-training toddler wears a shirt that snaps at the crotch, pull the front and back of the shirt up and snap the flaps closed over his shoulder.

SWING ONESIE UPWARD

SIDE VIEW

SNAP OVER *the* SHOULDER

FRONT VIEW

11 smart items to keep in the diaper bag

As you've probably discovered, to be truly useful, your diaper bag needs to hold a lot more than diapering supplies. Think of it as your survival pack. When properly stocked, it can save the day.

Beyond the basics, here are a few handy items you may not have thought to stash in your diaper bag.

1 Plastic over-the-door hook. Hang it on chair backs and restaurant changing tables to keep the diaper bag off dirty floors.

2 Dog poop bag dispenser and bags. A convenient way to contain stinky messes. Clip the dispenser to the diaper bag.

3 Glad Press'n Seal. I rarely recommend products by brand name, but Glad Press'n Seal plastic wrap is unique. It sticks to itself and other surfaces with amazing efficiency. If you're out of bags, use it to seal dirty diapers and clothes in a leakproof pouch. You can also use it as a travel place mat, a bib, or a clean surface for putting something down. (See also pages 140–141.)

4 Painter's tape. Use painter's tape to quickly babyproof and secure sliding drawers, seal toilet seats, or cover electrical outlets. (See also pages 52–53.)

5 Swim diaper (in warm weather). Outdoor fountains, sprinklers, a friend's kiddie pool. . . . When unexpected opportunities for water play happen, you'll be glad you've got a swim diaper on hand.

6 An extra shirt for YOU. After a spectacular blowout, your baby's probably not the only one who needs changing.

7 Headband or ponytail holders. For keeping long hair out of your face when you're changing your kid on the floor.

8 Laundry pretreating stick. Several brands of stain pretreatment come in pen or stick form. Toss one in your diaper bag to pretreat stains soon after they happen.

9 A bottle of water and a grown-up snack. You've probably got the kid's food and drink needs covered, but you need to keep yourself topped up and hydrated as well.

10 Sticky notes. Temporarily disable the autoflush sensor in public restrooms by covering it with a sticky note (see also page 88).

11 Cash. Having a few bucks stashed in the diaper bag will get you out of a surprising number of jams. Think: small snack purchases, parking meters, neighborhood bake sales, and so on.

Scrape poop out of diapers with a spatula.

Most diapering how-tos include the deceptively straightforward direction to "flush solids" before tossing soiled diapers into the wash or the trash. But baby poop doesn't just roll out of the diaper; it often needs more . . . *coaxing*.

Use a cheap plastic spatula to scrape diapers. Clearly label the spatula POOP (so it doesn't end up flipping anyone's hamburgers), and hang it on the side of the toilet with a removable self-adhesive hook. When you're done with scraping, flush the toilet, swish the spatula in the clean water (if necessary, clean it with a flushable wipe), then flush again.

ESSENTIAL TOILET TOOLS

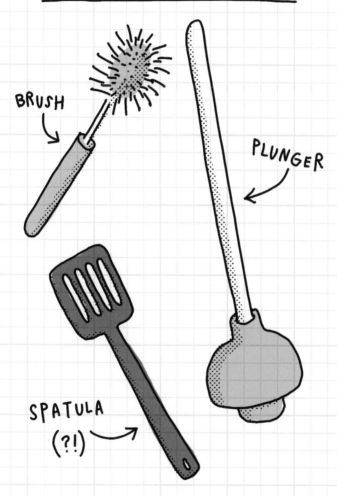

BRUSH

PLUNGER

SPATULA
(?!)

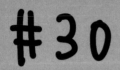

Puppy training pads protect the car seat from diaper blowouts.

Diaper blowouts are never pleasant, but when they happen while your baby's strapped into a car seat, you're in for a new level of *ewwwww....*

Keep messes contained by lining the car seat with a puppy training pad—a thin, disposable, waterproof pad pet owners use while house-training their dogs—before clipping your baby in. Puppy pads are cheaper than disposable changing pads, and they do the job just as well.

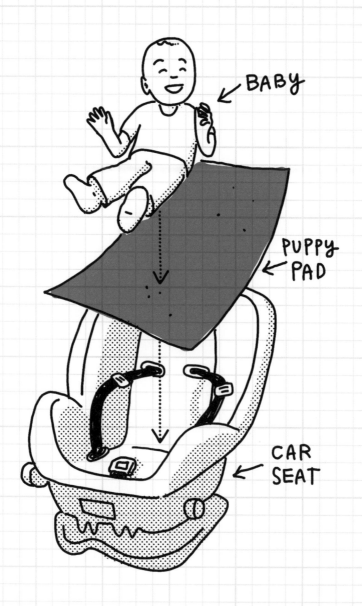

BABY

PUPPY
PAD

CAR
SEAT

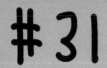

#31

Use a rubber band to remind you to restock the diaper bag with a clean outfit.

Murphy's Law of Diaper Bags states that the day you forget to pack a change of baby clothes is the same day your kid spews an unspeakable amount of . . . whatever.

The next time you're packing the bag, roll up a spare outfit, secure it with a rubber band, and stow it.

When you use the spare outfit, slide the rubber band onto your wrist to remind you to restock the bag when you get home.

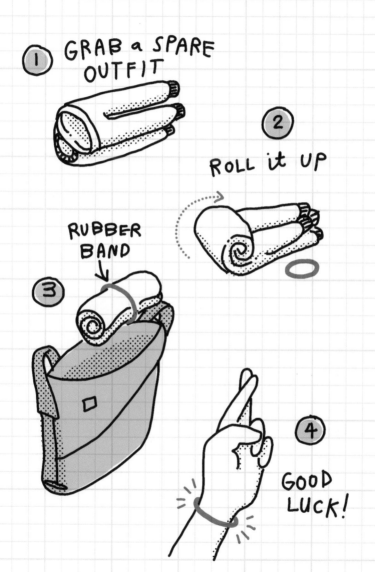

1 GRAB a SPARE OUTFIT

2 ROLL it UP

3 RUBBER BAND

4 GOOD LUCK!

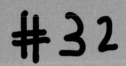
32

A panty liner turns regular underpants into training pants.

Disposable training pants can prolong potty training because they feel so much like diapers. Cotton training underpants are more effective, but they're also expensive when you consider how many pairs you need to keep on hand.

You might be able to skip the training pants by sticking a panty liner into regular children's underpants. While not leakproof (no training pants are), the panty liner protects clothing and furniture from small accidents, and your kid feels the wetness immediately, so learning happens fast.

YOUR KID

PANTY LINER

UNDIES

SHORTS

KEEP YOUR PANTRY STOCKED with BOTH QUART-SIZE and GALLON-SIZE

ZIP-TOP BAGS,

WHICH CAN BE USED for at LEAST a DOZEN TASKS BESIDES SEALING UP WET THINGS.

KITCHEN FUNNEL

RECIPE

PROTECT YOUR TABLET

PIPE CAKE ICING

ORGANIZE OUTFITS & SHOES for TRAVEL

MONDAY

NO-MESS "FINGER PAINTING"

WIPE-OFF COLORING PAGES

dry erase marker

SAND- & WATER-PROOF BEACH POUCH

MAKESHIFT SNOW BOOTS

INSTANT ICE PACK

for the cooler

or injury

KNEAD DOUGH with NO MESS

ROAD-TRIP CAR-SICKNESS BAG

TRAVEL POTTY

(do what you gotta do)

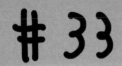

Line the training potty with toilet paper to simplify cleanup.

Most training potties come with a removable bowl to facilitate dumping and flushing of the contents. Easy with pee, trickier (that is, stickier) with poop.

Line the bowl with toilet paper to make cleanup a cinch. After your kid goes, tip everything into the toilet, give the potty bowl a quick cleaning with a flushable wipe, then flush everything away.

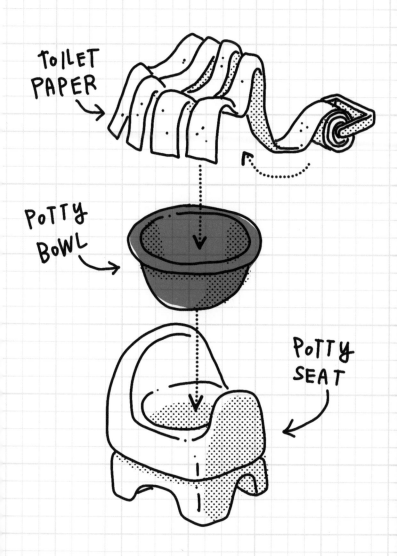

TOILET
PAPER

POTTY
BOWL

POTTY
SEAT

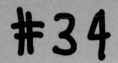

#34

Flatten the toilet paper roll to slow its rotation.

Potty training involves more than just learning to use the toilet. Kids also must learn to use toilet paper: how much to tear from the roll, the proper scrunching technique, and the mechanics of wiping.

Toddlers don't have the manual dexterity to control the spin of the toilet paper roll, so a lot of it ends up on the floor in a messy heap.

Before you put the toilet roll onto the holder, squash the roll flat. The uneven skipping will slow the spin.

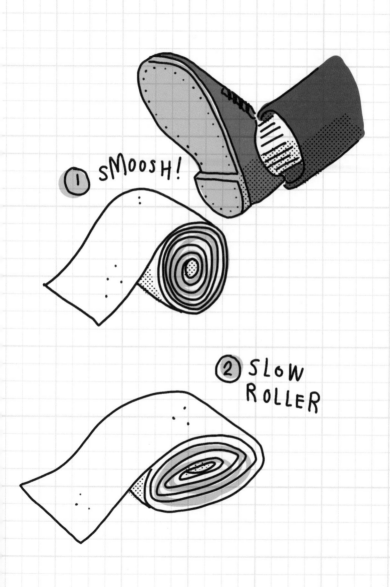

① SMOOSH!

② SLOW ROLLER

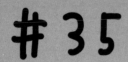

Trick the public restroom autoflush sensor by covering it with toilet paper.

Something about the automatic-flush toilet intimidates novice potty-users. Perhaps it's the loud, unpredictable vortex of doom swirling beneath their exposed bottoms?

Drape the autoflush sensor with toilet paper (or cover it with a sticky note or painter's tape) to trick it into silence while your kids do their business. Once they're finished, wiped, and on their way out of the stall, remove the paper and let the autoflush finish its job.

TOILET PAPER

SENSOR →

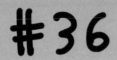

Use O-shaped cereal as a potty training target.

Little boys who've graduated to a regular toilet need practice perfecting their aim. Give him something to shoot for: a Cheerio (or similar cereal) tossed into the toilet bowl.

GIVE 'EM a TARGET

CEREAL OH'S

*DO NOT CONSUME AFTER USE.

Chapter 4
Sleep

New parents crave sleep as dogs crave:

- a. bacon
- b. cheese
- c. bacon-wrapped cheese
- d. all of the above

But you already know this, don't you? Your ability to sleep is closely tied to your kid's, so anything that helps her get shut-eye will help you, too.

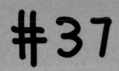

#37

Stash extra pacifiers in the corners of the crib.

If your baby sleeps with a pacifier, she may also wake up when it falls out of her mouth—a situation that will make you shake your fist at the heavens in frustration. Save yourself late-night searching time by stashing extra pacifiers in the corners of the crib at bedtime. If the pacifier falls out, confidently reach for a spare, pop it in, and head back to bed. Pretty soon, your baby will learn to roll over and grab her own pacifier, which, for some parents, marks the first full night's rest.

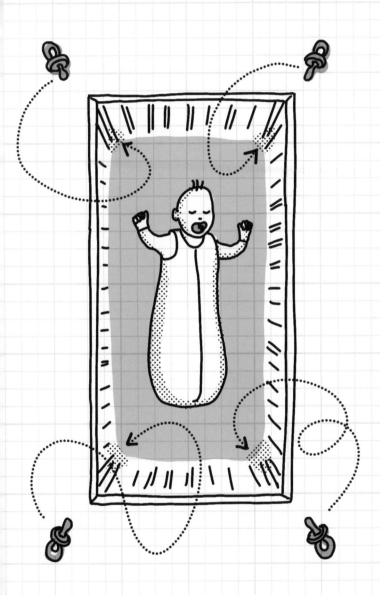

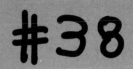

Muffle the door latch **with a rubber band.**

You tiptoe out of your sleeping baby's room, gingerly close the door, then CLICK! the door latch pops closed, the baby's eyes pop open, and naptime evaporates.

Prevent this painful scenario by looping a thick rubber band over one doorknob and twisting it to form an X. Depress the latch and tuck it behind the X of the rubber band, then loop it over the second knob.

#39

Exercise balls make great bouncers for fussy babies.

Is your exercise equipment lying neglected? You'll get back to your workouts soon enough. In the meantime, hold your fussy baby while gently bouncing on a fitness ball or mini-trampoline.

*DON'T TRY THIS at HOME

Put socks over footie pajamas to keep feet in place.

If your baby kicks her feet out of the pajama legs, slide a pair of baby socks onto her feet, over the pajamas. The combination of tighter socks and friction keeps the socks in place.

ELIMINATE FOOTIE CREEP!

SOCKS SAVE the DAY!

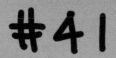

Use a pillowcase as a bassinet sheet.

If your newborn will spend the first few months sleeping in a bassinet, forgo the tiny sheets. Instead, slip the mattress into a standard-size pillowcase and firmly tuck any loose fabric underneath.

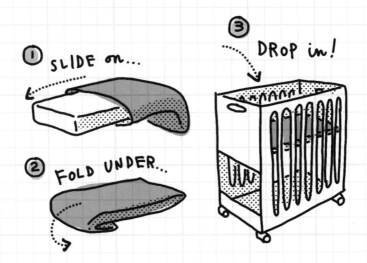

① SLIDE on...

② FOLD UNDER...

③ DROP in!

9 stuffed animal storage ideas

Stuffed animals seem to multiply like actual rabbits. There are several products designed specifically to solve the stuffed animal storage problem, but here are a few clever multipurpose options:

1 Underbed storage box. For kids who frequently swap out "sleep buddies," this is a good choice.

2 Hanging shoe organizer. Pockets hold collections of small animals and dolls. (See also pages 42–43.)

3 Mesh laundry hamper. A hamper has the benefit of being compact and portable.

4 Circular shoe rack. A free-standing shoe rack offers combination storage and display.

5 Empty beanbag chair. It can hold a *lot* of stuffed animals.

6 Hanging closet organizer. Put a few toys behind closed closet doors for less visual clutter.

7 Diaper stacker. Hang it in the closet!

8 Garment bag. Toss in lightweight toys and zip them out of sight.

9 Floor pillow cover. A pillowcase full of soft toys doubles as a fun lounging spot.

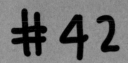

42

Buy replacement loveys and rotate them every couple of weeks.

A "lovey" is that treasured blanket or soft toy that moves into a special chamber of your child's heart. You can't control which item will become the lovey, but when it does, it has unique power. Once the lovey is identified, purchase multiples. Every few weeks, exchange the lovey with one of its replacements so they all wear and soften at similar rates.

Hopefully your kid's lovey will never get lost, but if it does, you'll have preapproved backups.

MULTIPLE LOVEYS

...SHARE the LOVE!

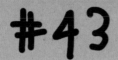

Crib sheets are quicker to change when you layer them with waterproof sheet protectors.

The beauty of this hack is most apparent after a 3 a.m. diaper explosion or an episode of the stomach flu.

Rather than making up the crib with a single fitted sheet and waterproof mattress protector, layer multiple sheets and protectors, lasagna-like. When disaster strikes, peel off the top sheet and protector to reveal a clean, dry sheet underneath.

BEDSHEET "LASAGNA"

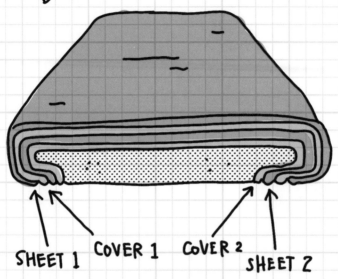

SHEET 1   COVER 1   COVER 2   SHEET 2

<u>WHEN DISASTER STRIKES</u>
TAKE a DEEP BREATH
& PEEL the LAYERS

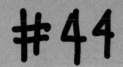

Help your kid climb into bed with a cookie sheet "step."

Moving to a big-kid bed is a milestone for both toddlers and parents. But even if your kid is ready to sleep in the bed, she may not be tall enough to climb into it. Make a built-in step stool by wedging a cookie sheet between the mattress and box spring, leaving about four inches exposed as a climbing ledge. She'll be able to get in and out of bed on her own.

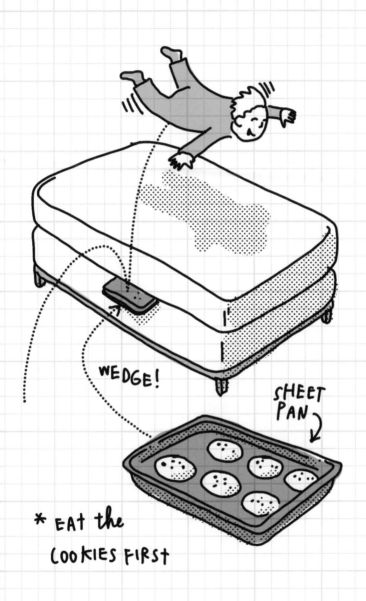

WEDGE!

SHEET PAN

* EAT the COOKIES FIRST

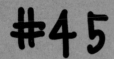
 # 4 5

Use a pool noodle to keep your kid from rolling out of bed.

If your kid's an active sleeper, those first few nights in a big-kid bed are nail-biters. Will he roll out of bed and hit the floor?

Wedge a pool noodle (or a tightly rolled-up towel) along the edge, between the mattress and the fitted sheet. The resulting bump is just enough of a barrier to keep your kid in bed through the night. (For more pool noodle hacks, see pages 180–181.)

HERE'S the PLAN:

FITTED SHEET

POOL NOODLE

MATTRESS

SWEET DREAMS!

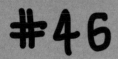

#46

Make a custom-fitted blackout window shade from a vinyl tablecloth or black felt.

If your kid leaps out of bed the moment a sliver of sunlight shows through the lined curtains, make your own blackout shades. Cut black felt or a vinyl tablecloth to match the size of the window, then use painter's tape to attach it directly to the glass. (It will peel off cleanly when you no longer need the shade.) Aluminum foil works, too, but isn't a great-looking option for street-facing windows. (For more vinyl tablecloth hacks, see pages 210–211.)

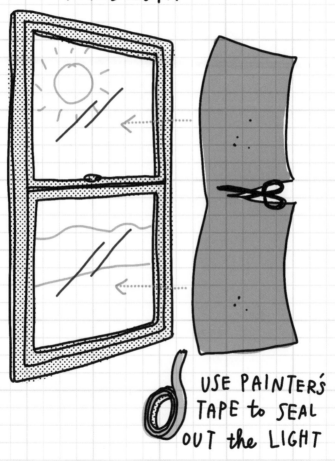

CUT UP a VINYL TABLECLOTH

USE PAINTER'S TAPE to SEAL OUT the LIGHT

7 pretend games you can play lying down

When you need rest but your toddler won't nap, try these games that have grown-up downtime built in.

1 Massage parlor. Lie on your stomach and invite your kid to pretend to be a massage therapist.

2 Hair stylist. Sit cross-legged on the floor while your kid brushes your hair.

3 Tattoo artist. Let your kid draw on your arms or back (somewhere you can easily cover up!) with washable marker.

4 Campout. Turn off the lights, unroll a couple of sleeping bags, crawl inside, and pretend you and your kid are sleeping in the woods.

5 Caterpillar cocoon. Lie on the floor and let your kid wrap you up in a blanket. After a minute, squirm around, then slowly emerge as a "butterfly."

6 Doctor. You lie on the examining table (aka the couch) while the "doctor" checks your temperature and other vitals, then looks in your ears and mouth.

7 Laser show. Turn off the lights, lie on the floor, and use a laser pointer to draw shapes and create effects on the ceiling. (This one works best at night.)

Chapter 5
Bath Time & Grooming

When I was a new parent, everyone raved about the deliciousness of "that new baby smell." What were they so excited about? My baby usually smelled like yogurt that had been left out of the fridge.

I eventually figured out how to keep my kid (mostly) clean and (somewhat) groomed, but it took practice.

You'll scale the bath-time learning curve soon enough. Whether it's a wipe-down with a damp washcloth or full-body soap-and-water immersion, you'll soon baby-bathe without a second thought. And you'll have a sweet-smelling kid to show for it.

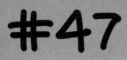

47

Turn cotton socks into baby bath mitts.

Wet babies are *slippery* babies. Get a more solid grip by cutting thumb holes into a pair of cotton socks. Slide them over your hands, thumbs out, then use them as wearable washcloths.

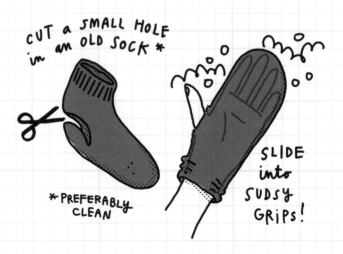

CUT a SMALL HOLE in an OLD SOCK *

* PREFERABLY CLEAN

SLIDE into SUDSY GRiPS!

7 multiuse containers for holding bath toys

Once your kid can sit up unassisted in the tub, the bath-time fun begins. Bath toys provide easy, reliable entertainment, but they can quickly take over the bathroom. Prevent "toy sprawl" by employing drip-dry containers that will continue to be useful once your kid starts showering.

1 Plastic milk crate or colander

2 Suction cup bath caddy

3 Plastic dish drainer

4 Plastic mesh wastebasket

5 Small plastic laundry basket

6 Hanging tiered vegetable basket

7 Mesh laundry bag (with a suction-cup hook)

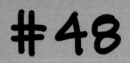
#48

Make your own easy-rinse foaming baby wash.

The next time you finish a bottle of foaming hand soap, rinse the container well and refill it halfway with baby wash and the rest with water. Close the bottle and gently tip it back and forth to mix. You'll double the life span of a regular bottle of baby wash, and the foaming wash is easier (and more fun) to rinse off.

SOAP

REFILL
with:

50%
BABY
SOAP

50%
WATER

GENTLY
SHAKE,
then GET
INSTA-FOAM!

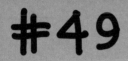

Rinse baby's hair with a watering can.

Small plastic watering cans are sold in the toy section as part of kids' gardening sets, but they're useful in the bath as well. Use a watering can to gently rinse shampoo out of your baby's hair.

FOR WATERING DELICATE FLOWERS of ALL KINDS

Smooth flyaway baby hair with a damp washcloth.

Eliminate baby bed-head: Dampen a baby washcloth, squeeze out most of the moisture, and smooth it over your baby's hair.

JUST a LITTLE WATER GOES a LONG WAY...

WHEN YOUR BABY INEVITABLY OUTGROWS the

BABY BATH TUB,

IT'S GOOD to KNOW YOU CAN STILL GET PLENTY of MILEAGE OUT of IT. HERE'S to SMART REUSE!

DOLLY SWIMMING POOL

OUTDOOR PET WASHTUB

ICE BUCKET for DRINKS

GARDENING TOTE

SOIL

SOAKING PAIL for STAINED LAUNDRY

MINI SANDBOX

BUBBLE-SOLUTION BUCKET for a GROUP

OUTDOOR WATER "TABLE"

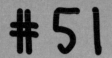

A dry washcloth keeps shampoo out of kids' eyes.

Even the "tearless" variety of shampoo stings. Avoid the problem altogether by holding a dry washcloth over or above your kid's eyes as you rinse the suds out. No more tears, for real.

Stretch thick rubber bands around bottles as nonslip grips.

Slippery shampoo bottles are easier to hold when you slide thick rubber bands around them—helpful when you're bathing your baby *and* when your child eventually bathes herself.

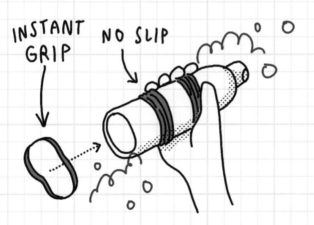

INSTANT GRIP

NO SLIP

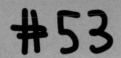
#53

Clip your baby's fingernails while she's in the front carrier.

Baby fingers are tiny. Baby fingernails? *Minuscule.* And they must be trimmed! Frequently! With a sharp metal clipper! While attached to floppy baby hands!

Hold your baby in a front-facing carrier while clipping her nails. She'll stay calm and relatively immobile, and you'll have two hands available to snip with precision.

(Some parents clip nails while the baby's sleeping, but that never worked for me. My kid was a light napper, and there was no way I was touching him after he fell asleep.)

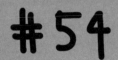

Mark the hot water tap with a red ponytail holder.

As your toddler gains bath experience, he'll want to experiment with those tempting handles, knobs, and taps. Remind him to avoid the hot water tap by wrapping it with a red ponytail holder. "Don't touch the red" is easier to communicate than "Don't touch the *H*."

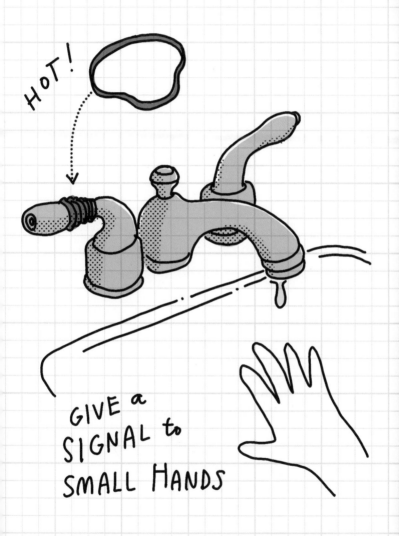

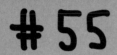
#55

Trim kids' bangs with nose-hair scissors.

Nose-hair scissors are ideal for trimming the bangs of a squirmy toddler because they're sharp enough to cut precisely, but the blades are small and have rounded tips.

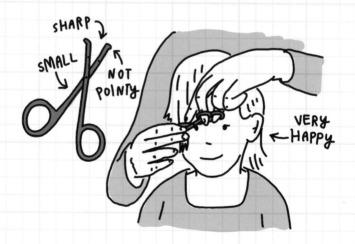

Chapter 6
Getting Dressed

I never knew that buying, organizing, washing, drying, folding, and donating my kids' clothes would take up so much brain space. With the wild cards of changing weather and constant growth, my standards for dressing my kids gradually dropped from "cute and tidy" to "fits and is mostly clean."

Getting (and keeping) your kids dressed is easier with just a little organization and a few good tricks.

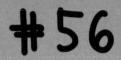
56

Designate a "next size up" drawer in the baby's room.

Set aside a drawer for clothing that's the next size up (an underbed storage bin beneath the crib also works well). As your baby grows (which sometimes seems to happen overnight), you can easily grab clothes that fit. And you won't forget about the long-ago-gifted outfits you've been waiting for your kid to grow into.

RIGHT NOW

SOONER THAN YOU THINK

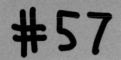

#57

Get nonsnap pants onto a baby.

Ever try to get floppy or kicking baby legs into a pair of pants or pajamas with no crotch snaps? Given how many diaper changes you have ahead of you, this baby-dressing hack is good to know.

Instead of struggling to scoot the pants over the ankles and up the legs, place your hand inside the bottom of one pant leg and pull it over your forearm. With your baby lying down, grab his foot and peel the pant leg off your arm and onto his leg. Repeat with the other leg.

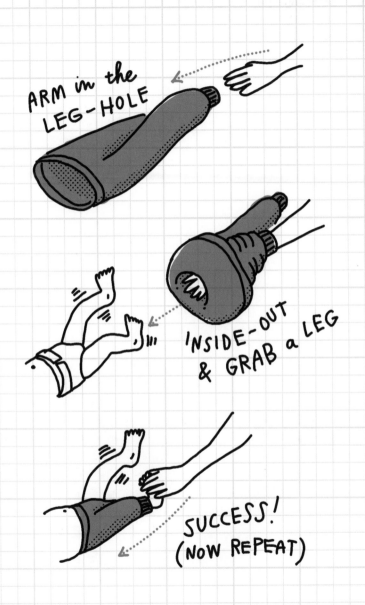

ARM in the LEG-HOLE

INSIDE-OUT & GRAB a LEG

SUCCESS! (NOW REPEAT)

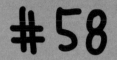

#58

Make baby leg warmers from an old sweater.

Baby leg warmers keep legs cozy without the diapering hassle that comes with pants. To make a pair, cut the arms off an outgrown kids' sweater or the feet off a pair of socks.

SNIP!
SNIP!

Glue down shirt collars on baby clothing.

Tack shirt collars and pocket flaps down using fabric glue. Clothes will look neater right out of the dryer. (And what do babies need pockets for anyway?)

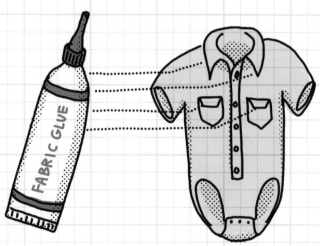

Reuse two-piece department store hangers as hat and mitten caddies.

Don't toss those awkward hanger sets that come with two-piece baby outfits. Use them to hang winter hats and mittens together.

Press small clothes with a flat iron.

Make short work of pressing ruffles, hems, bows, and cuffs by using a heated flat iron (a beauty tool used for straightening hair).

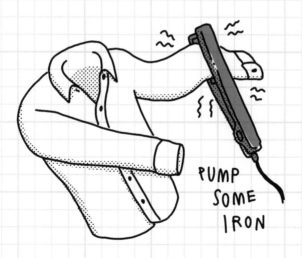

PUMP
SOME
IRON

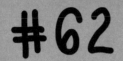
62

Tighten loose pants with a piece of elastic.

This hack for tightening loose waistbands is brilliant in its simplicity: a piece of elastic, a knot, and you're done. Slide a small piece of elastic through two side belt loops and tie it closed with a square knot. (If necessary, repeat on the other side.) If the pants don't have belt loops, use a double-sided mitten clip to cinch the waist tighter.

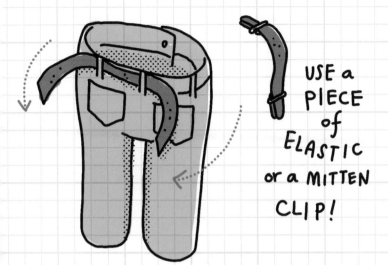

USE a PIECE of ELASTIC or a MITTEN CLIP!

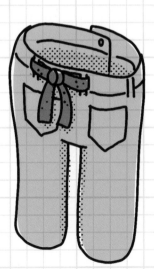

SLIDE THROUGH BELT LOOPS and TIE!

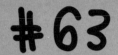

 # 63

Keep outfits rolled with a hair scrunchie so kids can more easily dress themselves.

Roll clothing separates into color-coordinated outfits (socks and all) and loosely secure them with a thick ponytail scrunchie. Dresser drawers stay neat, clothing changes are a snap, and older kids take the lead in dressing themselves.

SCRUNCHIES are BACK!

SLIDE 'EM ON

PRE-PLANNED OUTFITS!

ABLE to STICK FAST to ANY SURFACE, PULL AWAY CLEANLY, and FORM a WATERTIGHT SEAL WHEN PRESSED AGAINST ITSELF, GLAD BRAND

PRESS 'N SEAL WRAP

is for MORE THAN JUST FOOD. HERE are a FEW of ITS SUPERHERO-LIKE FEATS.

COVER a CUP and POKE a HOLE for a STRAW

QUICK PLACE MAT or CRAFT SURFACE

STICK DIRECTLY to CLOTHING for an "ART BIB"

TEMPORARY "WATERPROOFING" in the SNOW

LINE REFRIGERATOR SHELVES for EASY CLEANING

SEAL MEDICATION WHILE TRAVELING

child-proof!

PROTECT the CAR UPHOLSTERY

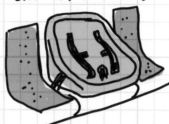

PLACE UNDERNEATH BOOSTER to KEEP DINING CHAIRS CLEAN

KEEP COOKBOOK PAGES SPLATTER-FREE

LINE PAINT CONTAINERS for EASY CLEANUP

PACK JEWELRY WITHOUT TANGLING

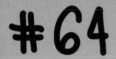

64

Temporarily shorten pants with first-aid tape.

"Hem" pajamas and pants with first-aid tape—it stays put during washes and is flexible enough not to irritate sensitive skin.

HOW to "HEM"

65

Clip tank-top straps together with a hair barrette to tighten.

Summer tops and sundresses are adorable, but the stringlike straps tend to slide and droop if they're too long. Clip straps together at the back with a decorative barrette.

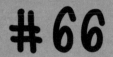

#66

Trace your kid's feet so you can shoe-shop on your own.

Every few months, stand your child on a piece of white paper (with grown-up assistance if necessary) and draw an outline around each foot with a pencil.

You can now take the template to the shoe store to determine the proper sizing.

67

Replace shoelaces with elastic to turn lace-up shoes into slip-ons.

Those toddler-size canvas sneakers sure are cute, but tying (and retying . . . and retying) shoelaces? Not cute.

Turn lace-ups into slip-ons by swapping out the shoelaces for lengths of ¼-inch-wide elastic. Thread the elastic through the shoe grommets, then knot the two ends together to secure. (Reinforce the knot with some superglue if it unravels.) Cut off excess elastic and tuck the ends back behind the tied "laces."

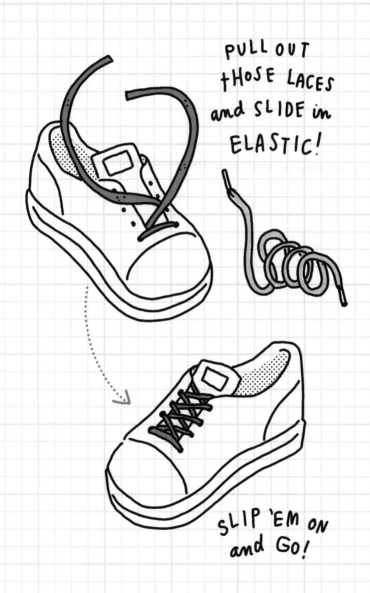

PULL OUT THOSE LACES and SLIDE in ELASTIC!

SLIP 'EM ON and GO!

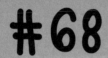

#68

Help kids put their shoes on the correct feet with a sticker.

Find a large, colorful sticker with a bold picture. Cut the sticker in half and place one half inside each shoe, and draw an "L" and "R" on the sticker halves with a permanent marker.

When it's time to put on the shoes, ask your child to "match up the picture." Doing so lines the shoes up with the proper feet, and helps teach left and right.

cut!

SPLIT!

stick!

6 ways to reduce or get rid of laundry stains

As a parent, you experience a whole new universe of clothing stains. Here are a few tips to help you bust through them:

1 **Reduce mealtime stains** by covering up your kid with a large T-shirt or cloth napkin.

2 **Keep laundry pretreating pens** or sticks wherever your kid gets undressed so you can tackle stains soon after they happen and before clothes go into the hamper.

3 **Scrub small stains** with a nailbrush or old toothbrush and a paste of baking soda and water.

4 **Fill a bucket** with a mixture of cold water and ½ cup color-safe bleach. Throw stained items in the bucket as they happen, then wash all the items together.

5 **Use the washing machine soak cycle.** Many stains simply need longer contact with detergent.

6 **Undress your kid** from the waist up to eat meals, and finish every meal with a good wipe-down.

Chapter 7
Food & Mealtime

During pregnancy, the umbilical cord took care of the job, but now you get to decide what, when, and how to feed your kid.

Providing sustenance for a small human can be both awesome and terrifying. Between breast-feeding, bottle-feeding, transitioning to solid food, and managing all the paraphernalia that comes with the job, there's a lot of pressure to do it "right." But, like so much else in parenting, how you feed your child is a personal choice, and there are many ways to do it well.

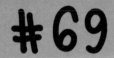

Turn a sports bra into a hands-free pumping bra.

For breast-feeding moms, having a pumped supply of milk at the ready is like money in the bank. But the pumping itself is both time-consuming and slightly bizarre. (Who knew nipples could do that?)

Turn a tedious chore into a self-care break. Buy an inexpensive, snug sports bra and cut a small hole in each cup just large enough to stretch and slide over the necks of the pump flanges. Put on the bra, hook yourself up, and your hands are now free to type, knit, or hold a book.

SNIP!

SLIDE THRU!

ATTACH!

Cut panty liners in half to make nursing pads.

Another "exciting feature" of early motherhood: leaky boobs!

Nursing pads—those absorbent pads you slide into your bra—handle the sudden drips, but for some women, panty liners, halved, work just as well at a fraction of the cost.

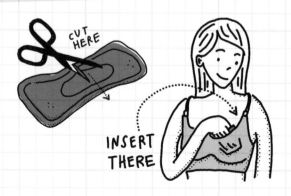

CUT HERE

INSERT THERE

Sort breast-milk bottles in six-pack cartons.

Keep refrigerated bottles of pumped milk organized by date in a cardboard six-pack carton. (Write the pumping date directly on the bottle with a dry-erase marker.) No more fridge spills, and the beer drinkers in the house will have something to talk about.

PUMP,
NO
DUMP

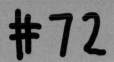

#72

Freeze breast milk in an ice cube tray for easy storage and quick thawing.

Skip those little plastic storage bags and pour pumped milk into a clean, lidded ice cube tray, and freeze. (Choose a tray with cubes that can easily slide into the bottle openings.) Once the milk is completely frozen, pop the cubes into a freezer bag and label with the date.

When you're ready to use the milk, place as many cubes as you need into a bottle and float the bottle in a container of warm water to quickly thaw.

POUR into a CLEAN TRAY...

FREEZE & STORE...

BOTTLE READY!

6 smart tips for better breast pumping

Most breast-feeding moms are intimately involved with a breast pump, and, for many, it's a complicated relationship: useful, but inconvenient. It's a lifesaver, but it's a struggle. Here are some wise tips from other pumping moms.

1 **Make** a hands-free pumping bra (page 152).

2 **Drink** water while pumping.

3 **Lean** forward and massage your breasts. (Let gravity help.)

4 **Close** your eyes, take deep breaths, and visualize a roaring waterfall. (No joke, some moms swear by it.)

5 **Buy** extra pump parts so you always have a clean set. If you can afford it (or can score a hand-me-down), keep a second pump at work.

6 **Store** expressed milk at room temperature for up to six hours (good to know if there's no refrigerator available).

Clean sippy-cup tops and valves with denture tablets.

For the occasional refresh (sippy cups can get funky), drop three denture tablets into a medium bowl of warm water. Add sippy-cup pieces, and soak for 30 minutes. Rinse the pieces under running water and let dry.

FOR CLEANING FALSE CHOMPERS...

...OR FUNKY SIPPY CUP PARTS!

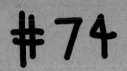

Mix formula in a shaker bottle.

Shaker bottles—those plastic tumblers with measuring lines and a snap-close spout—are popular with the fitness crowd for mixing up nutritional drinks. But they're also handy for mixing up multiple servings of formula.

SHAKE
SHAKE
SHAKE...

SHAKE that
BOTTLE

Use a divided formula dispenser as a dry snack cup.

Parents love divided powdered formula dispensers for preparing bottles while away from home. When your baby's past the formula stage, use the cup as a store-and-pour holder for small, dry finger-food snacks.

SPIN & SNACK

THAT SPONGY MESH MATERIAL that ADDS GRIP to FLAT SURFACES IS CALLED

NONSLIP SHELF LINER

and IT'S WORTH PICKING UP a ROLL, or FIVE.

SLIPPERY CHAIR PADDING

(so butts & boosters stay in place)

UNDER the CUTTING BOARD

ON HAIR BARRETTES to ADD GRIP

DRYING MAT for BOTTLES, ETC.

UNDERNEATH the TRAINING POTTY

JAR OPENER

(great for baby food)

UNDER THROW RUGS

UNDER SOAP & SHAMPOO BOTTLES in the SHOWER

← no slip!

UNDER PET FOOD BOWLS

BEHIND FRAMES (to KEEP ~~them~~ STRAIGHT on the WALL)

ADDED to a HANGER to KEEP CLOTHES from FALLING OFF

UNDER TABLECLOTHS

JIGSAW PUZZLE MAT

#76

Slide a sippy cup into an insulated beverage can holder.

Insulated beverage can holders fit several brands of spill-proof sippy cups, making them easier to grip and keeping them cool longer.

COZY UP with a COOZIE

GOOD VIBES ONLY

A suction-cup holder keeps sippy-cup valves safe.

Sippy-cup valves are easy to lose—or wash down the drain. Collect and dry them in a suction-cup sponge holder on the inside of the kitchen sink.

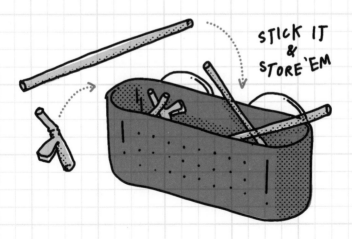

STICK IT & STORE 'EM

16 quick-fix dinner ingredients to keep on hand

A cranky kid can derail even the most well-organized meal plan. You need no-brainer ingredients on hand to quickly pull together a filling, nutritious meal. Think of this list as your dinnertime insurance.

1 Pasta. Various shapes of dried and frozen pasta can form the backbone of many simple, kid-pleasing dinners.

2 Bottled sauces. Good-quality sauces (soy, BBQ, marinara, curry) add instant flavor to grilled meats and vegetables.

3 All-purpose seasoning. A sprinkling of salt, pepper, and onion or garlic powder brings out the flavor in savory dishes.

4 Broth. Add chicken, beef, or vegetable broth (canned, concentrated, or cubed) to grains, soups, and sauces to boost flavor.

5 Canned tuna and salmon. Top salads with fish or form it into burgers.

6 Canned beans. Beans are a great inexpensive protein that are practically ready to eat (especially if there's salsa nearby).

7 Canned tomatoes. Many easy meals start with a can of tomatoes or tomato sauce.

8 Quick-cooking grains. Rice, quinoa, bulgur, and couscous can cook while you prepare the rest of the meal.

9 Olive oil. Use it in sautés and stir-fries and to dress salads.

10 Butter. A pat of butter and a pinch of salt adds flavor and richness to steamed vegetables, pasta, and rice.

11 Eggs. Scrambled, fried, or hard-boiled, eggs are a quick, versatile source of protein.

12 Chopped garlic and ginger. Keep a jar of each in the fridge to add fast flavor without tedious chopping.

13 Grated and shredded cheeses. Parmesan, jack, cheddar, and mozzarella all freeze well.

14 Assorted frozen vegetables. The quality is good, the price is right, and you don't have to wash or chop.

15 Quick-cooking cuts of meat. Have your grocery store butcher trim, cut, and wrap meats for you to cook right away or freeze.

16 Sausages and meatballs. Add to pasta sauce for a filling meal, or sauté and serve with BBQ sauce.

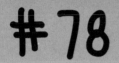

Cut food with kitchen shears.

Kitchen shears can cut spaghetti, halve chokable foods such as grapes or hot dogs, and even snip cheese sticks into bite-size pieces—all without dirtying a cutting board or fussing with a sharp knife.

Serve "samples" of new foods in an ice cube tray.

Your kid is wary when you serve new foods at mealtime, but gobbles up the bite-size samples at the store. Sound familiar? If so, try filling in an ice cube tray with tiny finger foods and serve them up!

TASTING MENU!

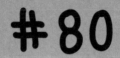

Use a shot glass as a toddler drinking glass.

If your toddler wants to drink out of a regular glass, let her begin with a shot glass or clean baby food jar. With less liquid to spill, they're easier for little hands to maneuver.

DRINKING GLASSES for LITTLE HANDS

Put the ketchup under the hot dog.

When your kid graduates to eating whole hot dogs, squeeze the ketchup onto the empty bun *before* adding the hot dog. Less mess on hands and clothes!

ASSEMBLY VIEW

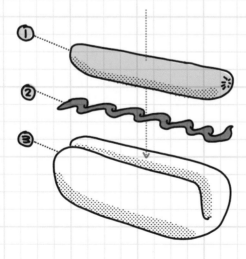

① ② ③

#82

Make sandwiches "inside out" to use up bread heels.

When I was a kid, my mom told me I had to eat the bread heels because "the crust is the healthiest part." It made sense (after all, the peel is the healthiest part of the apple, right?), and I dutifully polished off my sandwiches.

If your kid is savvier than I was, flip the bread heels so the crusty part of the bread is on the *inside* of the sandwich. Your kid probably won't notice.

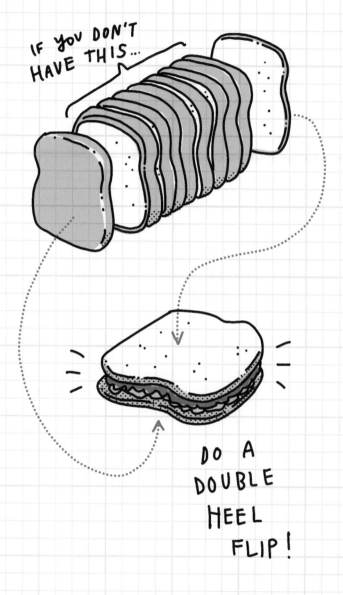

IF YOU DON'T HAVE THIS...

DO A DOUBLE HEEL FLIP!

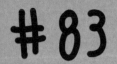

Cool hot food by adding frozen fruits or vegetables.

To cool food quickly, add frozen fruit or vegetables, ice cubes, or cold sauce. (Think frozen blueberries stirred into hot oatmeal, or refrigerated tomato sauce added to steaming pasta). Frozen items thaw, and cold sauce heats as it cools the hot food.

ICE CUBES!

HOT CHOCO-LATE!

FROZEN BLUE-BERRIES!

OATMEAL!

COLD PASTA SAUCE!

PASTA!

FROZEN PEAS & CARROTS!

CHICKEN NOODLE SOUP!

Clean the high chair with a baby wipe–wrapped toothpick.

Wrap the corner of a baby wipe around a toothpick and run it along hard-to-clean grooves. It's narrow enough to dig in, and the wipe solution dissolves the gunk.

GUNK CAN RUN, BUT it CAN'T HIDE

Chapter 8
Health & Safety

Family life is full of sniffles, ear infections, scraped knees, and other hazards we can't anticipate—and nothing's more exhausting or worrying than when your kid gets sick or hurt.

You can't protect your kids from every virus or sharp corner, but you can arm yourself with a few tricks for simplifying sick days. Anything that helps your child (and you) stay calm and rested will help speed healing so you can both get back to normal life (whatever that means) as quickly as possible.

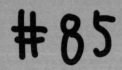

#85

Keep cabinet doors closed with silicone bracelets.

Looped around cabinet door handles, silicone bracelets work as lightweight locks—snug enough to keep a baby from opening the doors, but flexible enough for an adult to remove without hassle. No bracelets? Use ponytail holders or thick rubber bands.

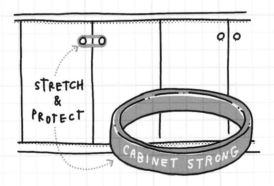

STRETCH & PROTECT

CABINET STRONG

Use a bottle nipple to dispense medication.

If it's hard getting your baby to take medicine with the built-in dropper, place your finger over the hole of a bottle nipple, pour the medicine in, then pop the nipple into the baby's mouth.

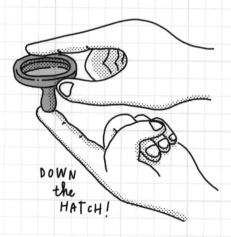

DOWN
the
HATCH!

A SUMMERTIME POOL FIXTURE, the

POOL NOODLE

IS INCREDIBLY VERSATILE. CUT it to
SIZE with a SERRATED KNIFE, and
PUT it to WORK ALL OVER the PLACE.

PLAYING-
CARD
HOLDER

GIANT LACING BEADS

SQUIRTING
SPRINKLER
to hose TOY

BASKETBALL HOOP

DOOR
STOPPER

CUSHIONING for SHARP
TABLE CORNERS & HEARTH
EDGES

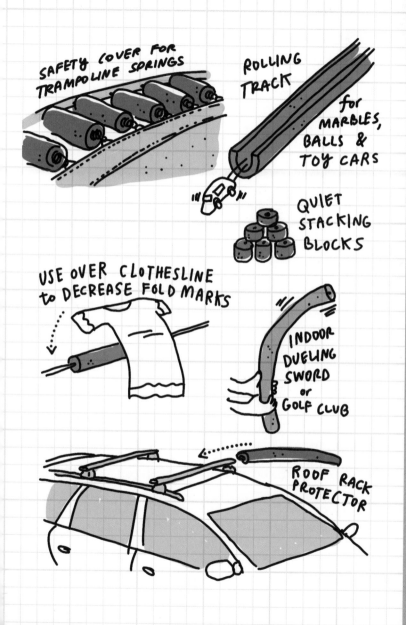

SAFETY COVER FOR TRAMPOLINE SPRINGS

ROLLING TRACK for MARBLES, BALLS & TOY CARS

QUIET STACKING BLOCKS

USE OVER CLOTHESLINE to DECREASE FOLD MARKS

INDOOR DUELING SWORD or GOLF CLUB

ROOF RACK PROTECTOR

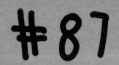

#87

Write medicine dosage schedules on the bathroom mirror to keep track.

Your baby's sick and needs X milliliters of medicine every Y hours for Z days. . . . Sounds like the setup for a math problem. Keeping track of the dosing schedule can confound even the most organized person, especially if your sleep is disrupted and it's a shared job.

Keep it simple by writing dosage amounts and timing directly on the bathroom mirror with a dry-erase marker, near the medication, so everyone's on the same page.

Contain dirty tissues with a tissue box trash can.

Use packing tape or rubber bands to bind an empty tissue box to a full one. Used tissues get stuffed in the empty box.

TAPE BOXES TOGETHER

STUFF DIRTY TISSUE into OLD BOX

Use a training potty as a vomit catcher.

Post-barf cleanup is so much easier if you keep the training potty nearby. The stable base will keep it from tipping and the removable insert is easy to empty and wash.

FOR MIDNIGHT EMERGENCIES

8 ideas for grown-up time that don't require a babysitter

You *need* a babysitter, because time away from your kids recharges the relationship batteries you don't always notice are running low. But when going out just isn't an option, you can still carve out some fun time with a friend or romantic time with your partner. Sure, you might get interrupted, but then again, maybe tonight's the night the kid will finally stay asleep.

1 Deluxe movie night. Make movie-watching more of an occasion by changing the venue (laptop in bed instead of couch and TV) or the snacks (popcorn and candy, pizza, an adult beverage?).

2 Light the fire and eat s'mores. You can toast marshmallows over a gas flame, or toast graham crackers, chocolate, and marshmallows together in a 400-degree oven for three to five minutes.

3 **Eat dinner together after bedtime.** Feed the kids a simple dinner, then have your own special meal after you put the kids to bed. Order takeout, break out the china and the candles, pour some wine, turn on some (quiet) music, and revel in an evening of uninterrupted conversation.

4 **Game night.** Board games and card games are more fun than you remember, especially if you browse the local game store instead of a toy store. Forget Monopoly and play something new. If board games aren't your thing, play video games or do a crossword or jigsaw puzzle together.

5 **Do a craft.** Getting creative and crafty together can be a blast.

6 **Stare at the stars.** After the kids are in bed, bring some blankets (and, if you like, the baby monitor) outside, then plop yourselves down in a cozy spot for some stargazing. You'll wonder why you haven't done it in so long.

7 **Make out in the car.** Unless you're interested in putting on a free neighborhood show, park in the garage.

8 **Early bedtime.** Put yourselves to bed right after the kids. Ignore the dishes, the to-do list, and the late-night television. (You decide what to do after the door is closed.)

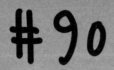
90

Fasten a clip to the bottom of the freezer pop package.

For some kids, there's one bright side of the stomach flu: the freezer pops they get to suck on for rehydration. But the pops tend to slide back down into their plastic coverings, making them tricky for little kids to manage.

Easy fix: Squeeze the pop out of the plastic, then fasten a bag clip, binder clip, or clothespin at the bottom of the package to keep the pop in place.

REHYDRATION STATION:

POP UP the ICE POP

CLIP— NO SLIP!

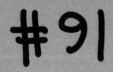

#91

Heal your child's chapped skin **with nipple cream.**

Got leftover nipple cream? Use it to protect and soothe skin that's raw from teething, tissue-wiping, and thumb-sucking.

HEAL SORE SKIN of ANY KIND

Chapter 9
Fun & Learning

Parenthood is a crash course in being a grown-up, but it also reintroduces you to the fun of being a kid. Making funny faces and bursting into song are legitimate ways to delight your child *and* demonstrate your fabulous parenting. *Playing is part of your job again*.

Even better: For little kids, the divisions between playing, working, and learning don't exist. Every moment of playtime teaches them about the world.

And the less time you spend managing toys and supplies, the more time you have for fun.

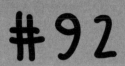

Use the open dishwasher door as a pouring surface.

Help your toddler practice her dexterity while minimizing the inevitable cleanup when she wants to "help" measure dinner ingredients. Set the bowl on the open dishwasher door, creating a low table surface for pouring.

MAKE a MESS: NO STRESS

Wash small toys in a mesh lingerie bag in the dishwasher.

If the LEGO bricks and plastic zoo animals are getting grimy, throw them into a zippered mesh lingerie bag and run them through the dishwasher (top shelf, air-dry).

LOAD & WASH

EVEN AFTER YOUR KIDS OUTGROW WIPES,
IT'S LIKELY YOU'LL STILL HAVE an EMPTY

BABY WIPE tUB

or TWO AROUND the HOUSE. HERE ARE a
FEW of MY ABSOLUTE FAVORITE USES:

ORGANIZE
ART &
SCHOOL
SUPPLIES

STORE
SMALL
PARTS
from
BABY
BOTTLES & SIPPY CUPS

TRASH
RECEPTACLE
for the
CAR

ORGANIZE
SPICE
PACKETS
in the
PANTRY

TACO
MIX

PLASTIC
BAG
DISPENSER

STORE
HARDWARE
& OTHER
SMALL
PARTS in
the GARAGE

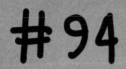
#94

Before painting, rub lotion on kids' hands for easier cleanup.

If you're brave enough to hand your kid a loaded paintbrush, save yourself cleanup time: Rub your child's hands with lotion so the paint will wash off more easily.

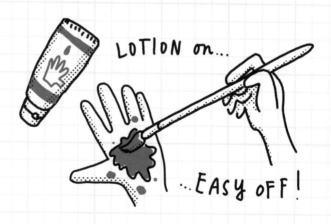

LOTION on...

...EASY OFF!

Store crayons in a plastic travel soap dish.

A rectangular plastic travel soap dish (sold at most dollar stores) is the right size and shape for holding 24 crayons. Not only can you get rid of the torn cardboard box, but the soap dish halves keep the crayons on the table.

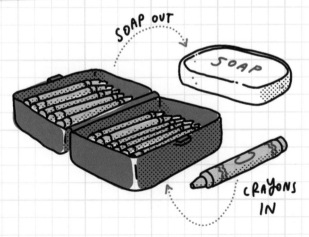

SOAP OUT

SOAP

CRAYONS IN

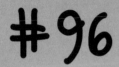

Turn a cleaning caddy into a portable art kit.

A plastic cleaning caddy keeps art supplies organized and makes them easy to carry to the table when it's project time.

Clean up glitter with play dough.

Glitter is universally adored, universally spilled, and then universally despised. But it's fun to turn a mishap into its own art project. Roll play dough over the glittery table for a clean table *and* sparkly play dough. WIN-WIN.

6 easy ways to display, organize, and repurpose your kid's artwork

The problem with your kid's art projects is that they're all so cute. (Or maybe they're not, but they're still difficult to throw away.) But what starts as a few scribbles during the toddler years grows into a deluge of art projects once preschool begins. The sooner you get ahead of the wave, the better.

There are ways to celebrate your child's artistic obsessions, reinvent the stuff that's not particularly special, and store the highlights for posterity. The more you edit, the more you enable the real masterpieces to shine.

Here are a few simple ideas for displaying, reusing, and preserving your child's art at home.

1 **Create a hanging art gallery in the hallway or garage.** Hang some wire onto which you can clip drawings and paintings (binder clips and wooden clothespins work well). Tossing old art becomes easier after it's had its moment on display.

2 **Use paintings and drawings for a decoupage project.** Decoupage is the process of covering an object with a mosaic of ripped paper and diluted craft glue. Decoupage a thrift store picture frame with bits of a colorful painting.

3 **Wrap gifts using your kids' art projects.** This is the perfect way to use up those big pieces of newsprint (and will delight the gift recipient!). Cut smaller art pieces into cards or gift tags.

4 **Laminate art to use as place mats.** You can buy a home laminating machine (surprisingly useful) or take original art pieces to the local office copy-and-print shop. Once laminated, art pieces wipe clean with a damp paper towel.

5 **Scan or take a picture of favorite art pieces and toss the originals.** If you like, go a step further and gather the photos into a book or calendar (easy to do online through any number of photo printing services).

6 **Store art projects in cardboard mailing tubes.** This way, everything stays neat and takes up a minimal amount of storage space. As the volume of art increases, buy a new tube for each year.

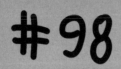

Skim the kiddie pool with a kitchen strainer.

Kiddie pools are a great summertime joy, but cleaning out the leaves, bugs, and grass clippings? Not so much. Skim debris from the water with a mesh kitchen strainer. Then snap a fitted crib sheet over the pool as a cover.

STRAINING the "KIDDIE TEA"

Turn the portable crib into a ball pit.

Play spaces filled with plastic balls and overexcited children *seem* like fun . . . until pandemonium and the gross factor set in. Make your own ball pit by filling a portable crib or kiddie pool with plastic play balls.

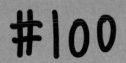

#100

Put yogurt or pudding in a zip-top bag for no-mess finger painting.

Take the pain (of tedious cleanup) out of finger painting by spooning yogurt into a zip-top freezer bag, squeezing out the air, and sealing and taping the bag shut. Lay the bag on the table, and your kids will have fun pressing the bag to make patterns.

For times when mess is part of the fun, spoon the yogurt directly onto the high chair tray for "finger paint" that's fun to eat. (For best results, do this activity right before bath time.) For more uses for zip-top bags, see pages 82–83.

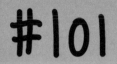

101

Contain small parts with a cookie sheet.

If your child loves to play with beads, LEGO bricks, shape tiles, or games with small components, set him up with a cookie sheet "play place mat." Toys stay contained, cleanup is easier, and chokable small parts are less likely to roll onto the floor where younger siblings may find them.

(This is a good technique for keeping crayons and markers on the table, too.)

CORRAL the MESS!

(MOSTLY)

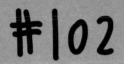

Turn an underbed storage box into a sandbox.

Building an outdoor sandbox takes time, skill, and dollars. But it's quick, easy, and inexpensive to fill a plastic lidded underbed storage box with play sand purchased at a home improvement store. You can move it with the shifting shade, and then cover it when playtime is over.

For an indoor version, fill the box with rice (easy to sweep or vacuum).

FOLDABLE, WIPEABLE, WASHABLE, and WATERPROOF, THERE'S a LOT YOU CAN DO WITH a LINED

VINYL TABLECLOTH.

KEEP ONE at HOME and ONE in YOUR CAR— YOU'LL BE SURPRISED at HOW OFTEN YOU USE IT.

INFANT PLAY MAT

CHANGING PAD

TRUNK PROTECTOR

(from dirty stroller wheels)

FORT COVER

PICNIC BLANKET

Extend the life of musical toys by leaving out the batteries.

Electronic toys can be just as fun without the batteries! Toddlers are none the wiser and will be *delighted* months later when you pop in batteries and the toy makes sounds.

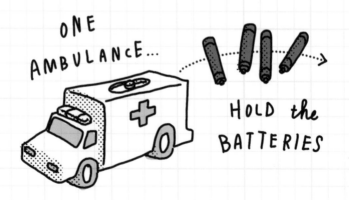

ONE
AMBULANCE...

HOLD *the*
BATTERIES

Limit TV time by starting shows in the middle.

You've got 15 minutes, but your kid wants to watch a 30-minute program. Avoid tantrums by starting the show in the middle. He's less likely to protest turning off the TV after the credits roll.

TRIM that SHOW in HALF

POPPYSEED AVE. EPISODE 2

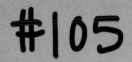

Define play zones in shared spaces with painter's tape.

Kids usually want to bring their toys to wherever the rest of the family is hanging out. Press blue painter's tape onto the floor to define a "toy zone" in shared rooms. It helps keep toys in bounds while teaching kids to respect the shared space—and also peels up easily should the "architecture" of the space need to change. For more ways to use painter's tape, see pages 52–53.

TOY-FREE ZONE

ANYTHING GOES

Manage electronics with poker chips and a kitchen timer.

"Screen time" is a source of both relief and frustration for many parents. Here's a way to manage and monitor it.

Get a set of plastic poker chips and a timer. Decide how much time a chip is worth. If necessary, designate a chip color for each activity.

Explain the new "electronics bank": Your kid receives or earns one or more chips every day. For each chip he pays you, he receives a certain amount of time in return.

Slide wooden puzzles into panty hose to keep the pieces together.

Cut the leg off an old pair of panty hose and stretch them around wooden puzzles to keep the pieces from falling out when storing.

STRETCH

Chapter 10
Travel & Outings

There's no longer such a thing as a "quick trip to the store" or a "relaxing vacation." Routine errands turn into epic adventures, and pleasure travel has its inevitable moments of pain (many parents joke about needing a vacation after they get home from vacation).

Sure, travel with kids is more complicated. But it's also full of wonder and surprise. By embracing the unpredictability and minimizing the hassle, you can maximize the fun of being out and about with your family.

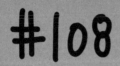

A backward cardigan or fleece jacket works like a car seat Snuggie.

Ever tried to buckle your kid into the car seat while he's wearing a winter coat? It's like wrestling with a small, irritable version of the Stay Puft Marshmallow Man.

Instead, buckle your kid into the seat without the jacket on, then slide the jacket over his arms so it covers his chest. He'll stay warm and comfortable, and you'll avoid the car seat battle.

FLIP THAT JACKET AROUND

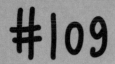

Throw towels over the car seat to keep it cool.

On warm days, car seat buckles get hot. Cover the seats with a couple of thick beach towels. The towels can double as blankets, pillows, picnic seats, cleanup tools, and upholstery protection.

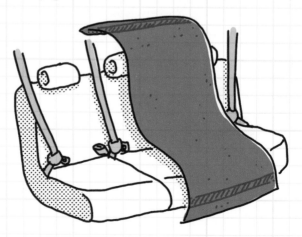

7 restaurant items that double as toys

Sooner or later, your kid will be *that kid* in the restaurant. When the toys or crayons you brought with you are no longer doing the trick, entertain your kid with common restaurant objects:

1 Stir sticks. Lay them on the table to form shapes, letters, and patterns.

2 Drinking straws. Scrunch the paper cover off the straw to make a springy "caterpillar." (Then add a few drops of water to make it grow!) Or twist it around your finger to make a curly spring.

3 Extra spoons. As soon as you're seated, ask for extra spoons. Bring them out for your kid to hold if she starts getting restless. (But keep your kid's temperament in mind: Some quietly play with spoons; others bang the table. Loudly.)

4 Menus. Babies love to turn the pages; give older kids a task—they can start identifying numbers and letters.

5 Napkins. Play peekaboo with babies and tic-tac-toe with older kids.

6 Paper cups. Stack them. Nest them. Use them as big ears or binoculars.

7 Cardboard cup sleeves. Turn them into superhero arm cuffs.

#110

Line your car's cup holders with cupcake liners.

Toys, wrappers, and rocks leave the cup holders full of dust, crumbs, and other detritus. Insert a small basket coffee filter or cupcake liner into each holder; simply remove and replace to clean.

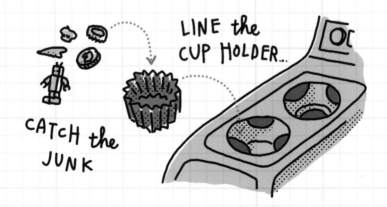

CATCH the JUNK

LINE the CUP HOLDER...

Use a mitten clip to keep loveys from getting lost.

If your kid likes to bring her lovey with her on outings, take measures to keep it from getting lost. Attach it to your kid's clothes using a mitten clip.

SHOW the LOVEY SOME LOVE!

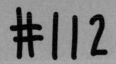

Use a wine bottle tote as a car organizer.

Car trips go more smoothly when you can quickly find and grab the toy or snack you need. A divided wine bottle tote is the perfect tool for the job. Its small, vertical compartments are just the right size to keep toys, art supplies, and snacks from getting jumbled together.

SWAP OUT the WINE to AVOID the WHINE

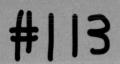

Strap ankle weights to the lightweight stroller to keep it from tipping.

Most of us have, in a pinch, hung bags from the stroller handles. The problem is that the weight of the bags can cause lightweight umbrella strollers to tip backward as soon as your kid climbs or is lifted out.

To solve the problem, strap ankle weights to the stroller's front wheels to balance and stabilize the stroller.

PUMP SOME IRON

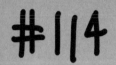
#114

Reduce static electricity on the playground slide with a dryer sheet.

If you've ever been the "catcher" for a kid coming down the slide, you know there's the possibility of a nasty static electric shock.

To reduce shocks, rub the slide and railings with a fabric softener dryer sheet, then have your kid sit on a second sheet as he slides down.

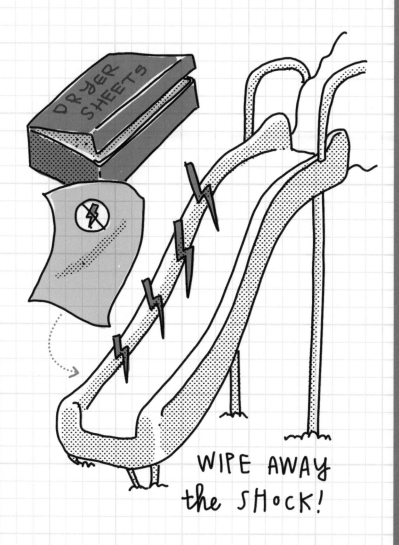

WIPE AWAY the SHOCK!

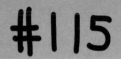

Fold the edges of restaurant coloring place mats to keep crayons from rolling.

Why are crayons cylindrical? One wonders, because they're always rolling onto the floor. When you retrieve crayons from beneath a restaurant table, you'll see things down there you'll wish you hadn't.

Here's a simple trick that works well enough to get you to the end of your meal: Fold up and crease one or more sides of the coloring page to create a little barrier between the crayons and the edges of the table.

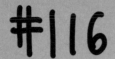

#116

Write your mobile phone number on your kid's belly.

If your kid tends to wander, this hack will give you some peace of mind as you travel to and through amusement parks, airports, parades, and other crowded places. Write your cell phone number *directly* on your kid's belly or arm with a felt-tip permanent marker.

If you'd rather not write on your kid's body, write your name and mobile number on a piece of first-aid tape and stick it inside your child's shirt.

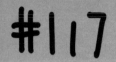
#117

Darken the crib with a hotel curtain or bedspread.

If it's dark and not too noisy outside, move the crib next to the hotel window and pull the room-darkening curtains around it. The curtains block light and noise coming from inside the room and create a calm environment for your baby to fall asleep.

Another strategy: Pull the hotel bedspread partway over the crib, blocking just enough light to help your baby settle down. (If hotel bedspreads creep you out, use a folded bed sheet or baby blanket.)

#118

Cover hotel room outlets with adhesive bandages.

Who thinks of childproofing on vacation? Improvise by covering the outlets with adhesive bandages from the first-aid kit (or front desk). Alternatively, use painter's tape (see pages 52–53).

KEEP FINGERS AWAY from SHOCKING SITUATIONS

Use glow sticks as travel night-lights.

If your kid feels anxious at bedtime in an unfamiliar, dark room, pack glow stick bracelets to use as wearable night-lights. Bedtime won't be nearly as scary.

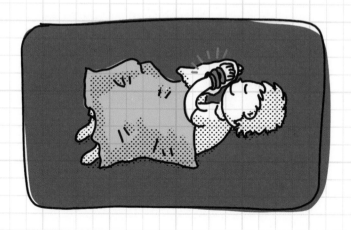

5 prepacked tote bags that streamline getting out the door

Turn tote bags into single-activity "kits" to organize stuff you misplace regularly or stuff you need to grab and go. A few examples:

1 **Return/exchange tote:** items you need to return, along with receipts

2 **Library tote:** library books to return

3 **Swim tote:** goggles, sunscreen, sunglasses, flip-flops, swim diaper, travel-size shampoo and conditioner, a comb or brush, towels, and a few bucks for a snack

4 **Giveaway tote:** clothes, accesories, and other items marked for donation

5 **Picnic tote:** paper towels and plates, plastic cutlery, napkins, and a vinyl tablecloth or picnic basket

Get sand off your kid's skin with baby powder.

Here's how to "wash" sand off your kid when there's no tap nearby: Use a liberal sprinkle of baby powder or cornstarch. The powder instantly dries her skin, and you can whisk the sand away with your hands.

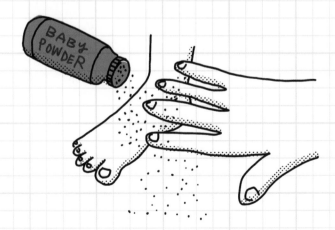

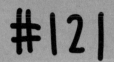

While swimming, keep valuables hidden in a disposable diaper.

You're ready to go swimming, but you don't want to leave your valuables unattended. Here's what you do: Wrap your keys and wallet inside a clean disposable diaper. Few petty thieves will be inspired to pick it up or investigate what's inside. Just be sure not to accidentally toss your "special package" into the trash as you leave.

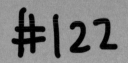

Use a plastic snow sled as a beach tow.

Let's go to the beach! Sounds simple enough until you remember you've got to get the kids, towels, toys, and food from the car to that perfect spot by the water.

The answer is a piece of winter play equipment: a plastic snow sled. Load up the sled with beach supplies and drag it across the sand, saving yourself several trips back and forth to the car.

YEAR-ROUND SLEDDING!

7 ways to keep kids entertained on a plane—without electronics

Kids have a knack for blowing through whatever in-flight entertainment you've brought within minutes of takeoff. Here are some ideas using supplies available in most airplanes.

1 **Make** hand puppets out of airplane sick bags.

2 **Search** for pictures of airplanes or puppies or flowers in the in-flight magazine.

3 **Draw** silly mustaches, eyebrows, and hats on faces in magazine ads.

4 **Explore** the route map at the back of the in-flight magazine.

5 **Ask** the flight attendant for a local newspaper or a new magazine to read.

6 **Request** a blanket for an in-seat "fort."

7 **Use** plastic cups and stir sticks from the drink cart (see page 223 for fun ways to play with these).

Chapter 11
Holidays & Special Occasions

Birthdays and holidays crank up the anxiety in even the most relaxed parents.

People blame lifestyle magazines for fueling our picture-perfect expectations, but I think there's more to it. We want our children to grow up with happy memories, so we put the pressure on Big Moments to roll out flawlessly. *I should put up a few decorations. I should bake the cake myself.*

But the best holidays and parties are filled with laughter and conversation and celebration. No one cares if the cake is store-bought and the decorations are makeshift (or nonexistent).

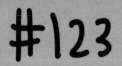

Cut cake with floss.

If you're cutting cake at a table full of excited children, skip the knife. Wrap a piece of unflavored dental floss around your fingers, lay the floss on top of the cake, then firmly and evenly press downward—cleaner, quicker, safer.

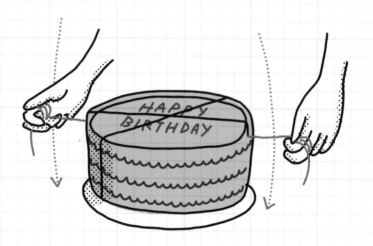

Store gift wrap neatly with a toilet paper tube "cuff."

Cut down the length of a toilet paper tube to form a cuff for rolls of gift wrap. The paper will stay neatly rolled while in storage.

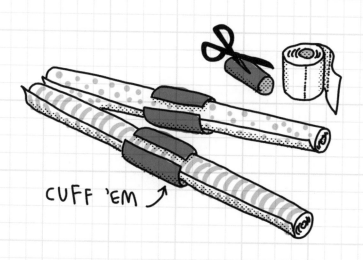

CUFF 'EM ↗

Use a muffin tin as a drink serving tray.

Here's a smart strategy for boisterous birthday parties. Place a plastic cup in each section of a muffin tin. Fill the cups in the kitchen, then serve party guests using a no-spill drink tray.

SERVE STEADY

Dye Easter eggs in a muffin tin.

Decorating Easter eggs will never be a mess-free project, but you can minimize the spillage by substituting a large muffin tin for wobbly bowls of dye. Each cup can hold a different color of dye.

DIP AWAY!

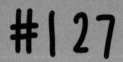

Dip Easter eggs into dye using a pasta fork.

Dipping Easter eggs into dye goes a lot faster (and more neatly) when you're using a tool other than your fingers. A pasta fork is the ideal shape for rolling an egg in dye then fishing it out while letting the excess dye drain away.

The rest of the year, use your pasta fork to retrieve small toys that have rolled under the couch.

PAIRS WELL
with PASTA
and EGGS

A TOTE and ORGANIZER ALL in ONE, a PLASTIC

LAUNDRY BASKET

CAN BE FILLED, TURNED UPSIDE DOWN, CARRIED, and SUBMERGED. HERE are a FEW IDEAS . . .

BATHTUB TOY CORRAL

GIFT CORRAL

TOY STORAGE

RECYCLING BIN

PULL SLED

PLANT PROTECTOR DURING BAD WEATHER

SUPPORT for BABY LEARNING to WALK

BEACH tote

FRISBEE GOLF GOAL

GARDEN VEGGIE RINSER

BASSINET

INDOOR TRAIN

CAR TRUNK ORGANIZER & TOTE

#128

Tie a ribbon to the bedroom doorknob to help a forgetful Tooth Fairy.

Build a reminder into your family's Tooth Fairy ritual. Tie a ribbon to your child's doorknob to signal when there's a tooth to retrieve. Then set a backup reminder on your phone.

Draw jack-o'-lantern carving lines with washable marker.

Make the carving process easier on yourself by using washable markers to sketch the jack-o'-lantern's face. Once the carving is done, the marker lines wipe clean with a damp paper towel.

EASY-ON
EASY-OFF

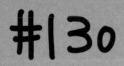

Hang outgrown baby shoes on the tree along with the ornaments.

If you can't bear to pass along the shoes and toys your baby has outgrown, give them new life as Christmas tree ornaments.

Wrap holiday gifts in pillowcases.

Skip expensive gift bags and wrap family gifts in pillowcases or cloth napkins to save time, tape, and trees. The fun is in the surprise (and in knowing there's barely any post-present cleanup).

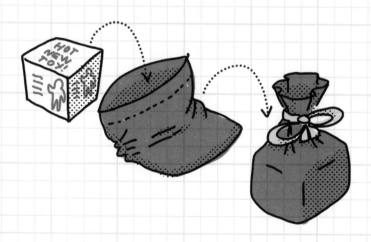

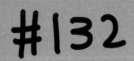

#132

Organize Christmas ornaments with beer case inserts.

The cardboard inserts inside beer cases look (and work) very much like ornament dividers sold in stores, and you can use them to keep ornaments organized and protected while in storage. Other options include egg cartons, the ribbed cardboard lining inside lightbulb packages, and plastic fruit packaging (fancy apples and pears sometimes come packaged this way—and, conveniently, right around the holidays).

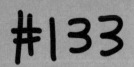
#133

Hang jingle bells from the Christmas tree as a "toddler alarm."

An eight-foot-tall evergreen decorated with pretty, shiny balls and twinkly lights suddenly appears in the family room. What self-respecting toddler *wouldn't* investigate?

Rather than fight a losing battle to keep your child away from the tree, hang oversize jingle bells (the kind sold in craft stores for decorating wreaths) on the tree's lower branches. That way, when your kid gets curious, you'll hear the ringing and can intervene.

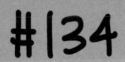
#134

Use a can opener and nail clippers to open toy packaging.

Nothing inspires "unwrapping rage" like the rigid plastic clamshell packaging and antitheft twist ties protecting new toys. When faced with diabolical packaging, grab a manual can opener and nail clippers.

Roll the edges of the packaging between the blades of the can opener, then snip the antitheft wires with the nail clippers.

6 tips for working with a neighborhood babysitter

Responsible kids in your neighborhood need a job and you need a break. Here's how to make it happen.

1 Start local.
Babysitting requires trust on all sides. Reach out to kids (and parents) you already see day-to-day. Bonus: Babysitters who can walk themselves home are the BEST.

2 Do a practice run.
Start with an hour or two while you're home. Everyone gets to know each other, and no one has to put anyone to bed.

3 Make plans via text. Be sure to text after school hours.

4 Text a same-day confirmation.
Open and frequent communication is always appreciated.

5 Have everything accessible.
Diaper bag stocked. Extra key. Emergency numbers. Snacks and meals for your kids and the sitter. Pajamas and a change of clothes.

6 Pay well. Ask around for the going rate, and pay at the high end of the scale.

Acknowledgments

This book is the result of more than ten years of conversation with thousands of people. The magnitude of friendship, mentorship, and generosity I've received as a result of the Parent Hacks blog is nothing short of remarkable.

I owe my deepest thanks to the readers of ParentHacks .com. When I shouted my thoughts and questions into the void, you answered, and when I most needed a community, you were there. This will always be a miracle to me.

The hardest part of writing this book was choosing which parent hacks to feature. The process was painstaking and took months, but after sifting through thousands of hacks, we finally settled on our favorites. A special thank-you to the superstar contributors of these hacks, whose first names (and/or screen names) appear on the inside covers.

Many of my dear friendships began with a single email or comment on a blog. What started as a group of us sharing stories blossomed into a vital community of writers, artists, and creators. This community has carried me for years with laughter, support, and tomfoolery. Big love to: Jessica Ashley, Gabrielle Blair, Alice Bradley, Kristen Chase, Amy Allen Clark, Catherine Connors, Anna Fader, Heather Flett, Meagan Francis, Doug French, Liz Gumbinner, Jeannine Harvey, Christine Koh, Emily McKhann, Whitney Moss, Cooper Munroe, Magda Pecsenye, Kyran Pittman, Gretchen Rubin, Karen Walrond, Ginny Wolfe, and Rebecca Woolf. I wish I could list every person who's inspired me.

To the organizers of the conferences that sparked collaboration and friendship: Lisa Stone, Elisa Camahort Page, and Jory Des Jardins (BlogHer); Laura Mayes and Carrie Pacini (Mom 2.0 Summit); Alli Worthington, Barbara Jones, Paula

Bruno, and Megan Jordan (BlissDom); Maggie Mason and Laura Mayes (the Broad Summit and Camp Mighty); Stacey Ferguson (Blogalicious); Jyl Johnson Pattee and Rachel Herrscher (Evo); and Chris Guillebeau (World Domination Summit).

I also want to thank my early mentors and supporters: Brenda Kienan (my first book editor), Tim O'Reilly of O'Reilly Media, Cory Doctorow of BoingBoing.net, Dave Pell of NextDraft.com, Dina Freeman of BabyCenter.com, and John Battelle of Federated Media.

My relationship with Workman Publishing has felt fated from Day One. I am so grateful to my incredible team: my editor Megan Nicolay, designer Jean-Marc Troadec, publicity and marketing geniuses Selina Meere, Jessica Wiener, and Noreen Herits, Publisher Susan Bolotin, as well as Kate Karol, Claire McKean, and Liz Davis. Special thank-you to Workman authors Austin Kleon and Jessica Hagy for camaraderie and advice— and to former Workmanite Netta Rabin for championing this book (and to Morgan Shanahan and Mike Spohr of Buzzfeed Parents for inspiring Netta to find me).

Adrienne Jones and Kris-Ann Race helped me pull together early versions of the manuscript. Thank you both for helping me through an especially overwhelming part of the process with superhero-like fortitude and encouragement.

I'm lucky to have Craighton Berman's illustrations gracing these pages, bringing *Parent Hacks* to life with energy and humor.

A huge thank-you to Josh Getzler of Hannigan Salky Getzler Agency for unflagging support, wisdom, and cheerleading.

Finally, I want to thank my family. I can never thank them enough. My parents and parents-in-law, for whom I'm forever grateful. My husband, Rael, who is beside me in every way and usually making me laugh. And my kids, Sam and Mirabai, who were the glorious start of all this, and who continue to fill me with wonder every day.